THE CONTEMPORARY CHALLENGE OF ST. TERESA OF AVILA

An introduction to her life and teachings

LEONARD DOOHAN

ISBN 978-0-9910067-8-6

099100678X

ABBREVIATIONS OF THE WORKS OF ST. TERESA OF AVILA

L. The Autobiography of St. Teresa of Avila

W. The Way of Perfection

C. The Interior Castle

F. The book of the Foundations

ST. Spiritual Testimony

S. Soliloquy

The cover photo was taken by my wife Helen. The statue of St. Teresa is located outside one of the great gates to the city of Avila

The Author

Dr. Leonard Doohan is Professor Emeritus at Gonzaga University, Spokane. He has written 24 books and many articles and has given over 350 workshops throughout the USA, Canada, Europe, Australia, New Zealand, and the Far East. Doohan's recent books include *Spiritual Leadership: the Quest for Integrity* (2007), *Enjoying Retirement: Living Life to the Fullest* (2010), *Courageous Hope: The Call of Leadership* (2011), *The One Thing Necessary: The Transforming Power of Christian Love* (2012), *Spiritual Leadership: How to Become a Great Spiritual Leader—Ten Steps and a Hundred Suggestions* (2014), *Ten Strategies to Nurture Our Spiritual Lives (2014)*, and *Rediscovering Jesus' Priorities (2014)*. Doohan has given courses and workshops on John of the Cross all over the world and his published tapes have been used throughout the English speaking countries.

Visit leonarddoohan.com

Books on the writings and spirituality of St. John of the Cross by Leonard Doohan:

The Contemporary Challenge of John of the Cross

John of the Cross: Your Spiritual Guide

The Dark Night is Our Only Light: A Study of the Book of the *Dark Night* by John of the Cross

John of the Cross—The Spiritual Canticle: The Encounter of Two Lovers. An Introduction to the Book of the *Spiritual Canticle* by John of the Cross

John of the Cross: *The Living Flame of Love*

A Year with St. John of the Cross: 365 Daily Readings and Reflections

These books are available from amazon.com

Table of Contents

Introduction

In 2015 we celebrated the five hundredth anniversary of the birth of St. Teresa of Avila. It was a special year for anyone who has been guided by the spirituality and teachings on prayer of Saint Teresa. My wife and I had the opportunity of traveling throughout Spain and seeing signs of celebration in every city and town. We have visited most of the places connected with Saint Teresa including several of the monasteries she founded —St. Joseph's in Avila, her first foundation; Our Lady of the Annunciation in Alba de Tormes, where she is buried; St. Joseph's in Segovia, near to John of the Cross' monastery where he is now buried; and others in Beas de Segura, Seville, Salamanca, Toledo, and Soria. We will always remember our visit to Medina del Campo and the monastery of St. Joseph's, Teresa's second foundation after St. Joseph's in Avila. There the Mother Prioress invited us into the enclosure so that we could see the tomb of John of the Cross' mother, Catalina Alvarez. The whole of Spain celebrated Teresa's great anniversary event, but Avila was alive with the presence of "La Santa."

This book is an introduction to the life and teachings of the Saint. It is a collection of notes and reflections taken from material I have presented in courses and workshops on St. Teresa over many years and in many countries to people from all walks of life who see Teresa's teachings on prayer as the vision and guidance they long for. This book on *The Contemporary Challenge of Saint Teresa of Avila*, is an introduction to her life and writings and readers should use it as a companion to the careful and prayerful reading of Teresa's own writings. It is in no way a substitute for reading her works; in fact I have rarely quoted from her writings, insisting that readers must encounter them for themselves. I hope these notes and reflections will introduce readers to this giant in the history of spirituality and one of the greatest teachers of prayer that the world has ever known.

This book is a companion to an earlier book, *The Contemporary Challenge of St. John of the Cross* which was used extensively by individuals and groups as an introduction to St. John of the Cross' life and teachings. It was also used by many in formation programs. This current book on Teresa may well fulfill similar goals.

Chapter One

The life of Teresa of Avila

We begin our reflections on the contemporary challenge of Teresa of Avila by looking at the major steps in her life. We immediately find a restlessness and a hunger for God that sometimes she pursues and then loses interest as she gets distracted by all kinds of secondary issues and values. Teresa was over forty before she made a resolute commitment to respond to God's call within her. Fortunately for us Teresa shares with honesty and simplicity the ups and downs of her life and the gradual process of growth in her dedication to God. In her experience of discovery of God's call and her slow and at times reluctant giving of herself to God, we find someone with whom we can identify. In spite of her slow start and years of set-backs, Teresa becomes a spiritual guide for us all, a renowned teacher of prayer, and a doctor of the universal Church. Let us spend a little time getting to know this extraordinary woman, her ordinary early life, and her universal appeal.

Teresa of Avila's early life (See *Autobiography*, chapters 1-3)

Teresa de Ahumada was born on March 28th 1515. Her mother, Doña Beatriz de Ahumada, was the second wife of Don Alonso Sánchez de Cepeda. Teresa was the third of ten children from this second marriage, and there were two other children from Alonso's first marriage. Don Alonso's father was a merchant in Toledo, a Jewish *converso*, who had accepted the humiliating penances and public degradation required of Jews for acceptance into the Christian society of sixteenth century Spain. Once accepted, he had moved his family to Avila to begin a new life. His son, Alonso was just fourteen at the time.

When Don Alonso and his family lived in Avila, Spain was not the united country it is today. True, the larger parts of Spain had been united by the marriage of Isabella of Castile and Ferdinand of Aragon in 1469, who had then gone on to re-conquer the south and especially Granada from the Moors in 1481-1492, earning for themselves the title "Catholic Monarchs." While establishing a unity not previously seen, each part of Spain remained independent and viewed others as foreigners. The Catholic Monarchs had also expanded Spain's powerful empire in the New World (1492), including Mexico (1519), and Peru (1531-33). Religious unity was seen as part of political unity and the Inquisition was authorized in 1478 to enforce religious uniformity. Later, all residents of Spain were forced to be Christians, including the Moors of Granada (Moriscos) and Jews throughout the nation. As a result of these forced conversions, in 1568 a savage rebellion broke out between the Christians and Moriscos of Andalusia.

In 1516, a year after Teresa's birth, Charles I succeeded his grandfather, Ferdinand, and in 1519 became Charles V, Holy Roman Emperor, whose lands included Spain, Netherlands, Austria, Southern Germany, and Italy. In 1556, after his father's abdication, Philip II became king of Spain and the Spanish territories overseas. He moved his court from Toledo to Madrid in 1560. Teresa lived during all these tumultuous times, including the time of Philip II (1556-1598), the golden age of Spain. This was a time of imperial expansion but also of great development in art, literature, architecture, social, political, and religious life. Spain's empire extended around the world, universities increased in number and importance, many of Europe's greatest scholars and artists were Spanish, and religious renewal was widespread.

Teresa spent her first sixteen years at home, formed by the care, love, and Christian dedication of virtuous and God-fearing parents. Her father was an example of virtue, charity to the poor, and compassion to the sick and underprivileged. Her mother was an example of all that was expected of a dedicated Christian woman in those days. By the time Teresa was fourteen, her mother had born nine other children, endured sickness, many difficulties of life, and constant pregnancies and motherhood, and she died on November 24th, 1528, at just thirty-three years old. By the time of Doña Beatriz's death, Teresa was beginning to move away from the piety and virtue previously shared with her brothers and sisters in the happy and virtuous environment created by her parents. Her mother had sought escape from her many burdens in reading books of chivalry, adventure, and romance, and Teresa joined her in these distractions, hiding them from her disapproving father. By the time she was thirteen, Teresa was a different young lady, given to personal vanity, frivolous relationships, adolescent fantasies, and the development of her feminine qualities. After her mother's death and the marriage of her sister, Teresa took over the management of her father's home, and proved herself very competent in administering it and handling family finances. At the same time, her frivolity and adolescent crisis became too much for her father to control, and he decided to send her to a boarding school just a few blocks from their home, where he hoped the Augustinian nuns of St. Mary of Grace might be able to bring focus and maturity to his wayward daughter. While having no desire to become an Augustinian nun and less attraction to enter marriage with the burdens she had seen her mother endure, Teresa did find some sense of direction in prayer through the care and guidance of one of the nuns, Doña Maria Briceño. However, after eighteen months at St. Mary of Grace, Teresa was sent home because of growing concerns about her health.

Teresa enters the convent of the Incarnation (See *Autobiography*, chapters 4-8)

Later, when Teresa showed some signs of improving health, her father sent her to spend some time with her sister who lived about a day's travel from Avila. Along the way Teresa stopped to visit her uncle, Don Pedro de Cepeda, who after his wife's death had given himself to a more intense spiritual life. He introduced Teresa to spiritual writings, notably Francis of Osuna's *Third Spiritual Alphabet* and the *Letters of St. Jerome*. His encouragement and spiritual challenge helped Teresa return to values of her earlier life, and this together with a growing fear of hell brought Teresa back to thoughts of entering religious life. She struggled with this idea for three months until she became firm enough in her resolution that she told her father of her wishes and decision. However, he refused permission. Nevertheless, in spite of an intense sense of separation, Teresa quietly left home on November 2nd 1536 and asked to join the Carmelite convent of the Incarnation. She was twenty-one years old. Teresa was professed two years later, in 1538, with the acceptance of her father who provided her with a dowry sufficient to assure her of private living quarters in the monastery.

The Incarnation had been founded in 1479 and was the largest Carmel in Spain, with about one hundred and forty nuns—some writers suggest up to two hundred. If we add the staff and some nun's relatives who also lived in the convent, there were well over two hundred people in the convent that was definitely not built for such a large number. In fact, several little girls also lived there, too young to be considered novices—Father Gracián's sister was only eight, and Teresa's niece, Teresita, was practically raised in Teresa's cell. The Incarnation was not an enclosed convent, and nuns often left for a variety of reasons, as did Teresa—their absence no doubt helping the monastery's problem of overcrowding. The nuns' primary religious duty was the solemn vocal recitation of the divine office in Latin which the nuns would not have understood. There was no emphasis on formation to mental prayer. In fact, Teresa acknowledges that she really did not know how to pray until she read Francis of Osuna's *Third Spiritual Alphabet* which her by her Uncle Don Pedro de Cepeda had given to her.

Prior to 1540, religion in Avila centered on wealthy, powerful families and their endowment of churches, chaplaincies, and so on, where religious communities prayed for these families and their extensive dynasties. The prayer was always vocal, out-loud so everyone could verify the obligation was fulfilled. After 1540, there was a move to mental prayer and personal conversion, and Teresa fitted in with this movement.

Teresa settled into monastic life quite quickly and smoothly. However, soon after her profession Teresa became seriously ill, and with doctors in Avila offering no hopes for a cure, her father sent her to her sister's house to await an opportunity to visit a famous quack healer who lived nearby. The three months of painful "cures" only made Teresa's health decline and became part of a five year period of suffering and painful self-conflict. The so-called "cures" never helped Teresa. In fact, she got worse, and in August 1539 she fell into a coma for three days, and those around her thought she was dying. She received the last rites, and at the Incarnation they even dug her grave. Teresa survived and returned to the Incarnation where she suffered paralysis for three years. In fact, she was a confirmed invalid at twenty-five and would suffer for the rest of her life. During all her years of illness Teresa showed continued interest in spiritual growth, conformity to the will of God, frequent Confession and Communion, and a desire for solitude. But she also continued in self-doubt, a lack of direction, and an inability to deal with the fundamental needs in mental prayer. So, she entered a period of difficulty in prayer, caused by a lack of understanding of what was happening in prayer. This was intensified by the lack of a knowledgeable spiritual director. Moreover, Teresa was overcome with confusion and discouragement that led to half-hearted efforts on her part. Teresa tells us that this painful period lasted about eighteen years.

Rather than transform the challenging situation Teresa allowed her commitment to weaken, and instead she stressed the outward practices of community, interaction with friends from outside the monastery, and pleasant society conversation and recreation. Moreover, she neglected the continuing call to mental prayer. Thus, she kept up appearances and was appreciated for her outward devotion but lacked the inner transformation she really longed for. The distractions and worldly interests led her away from spiritual growth and into crisis. Teresa ended up abandoning prayer altogether for at least a year and a half while at the same time hypocritically giving her father guidance in prayer. When he became aware of Teresa's deceit he lost patience in waiting for her frivolous encounters to finish and eventually he stopped visiting her. Later, her father became very ill and Teresa left the convent to care for him. His illness lasted only a short time and he died on Christmas Eve, 1543. Teresa and her father had become very close in later years and she felt intense sorrow at his passing.

Teresa returns to prayer (See *Autobiography*, chapters 9-10)

Following her father's death Teresa began to feel that God was drawing her back to prayerful union. At times she seemed torn between God's invitation and merciful love and her own reluctance and half-heartedness. However, one day she saw a statue of "ecce homo" that had been brought to the monastery for a devotional celebration. This provoked a sense of deep sorrow at her own failings and an appreciation of the sufferings the Lord endured for love of her. Teresa saw this experience as the beginning of a renewed commitment to

spiritual growth. It also led Teresa to a simple method of
reflection on the Lord's suffering that led her into prayer,
although she remained tormented by constant distractions.
These positive reinforcements in dedication were strengthened
by her reading of *The Confessions of St. Augustine*. Teresa saw
herself in Augustine's conversion and began to spend more
time in prayer, and she began to receive the Lord's favors. This
was a time when Teresa appreciated both the Lord's generosity
in the many blessings she received and also saw how people
could help themselves in the development of their prayer. The
gradual recommitment to prayer and spiritual growth that
began with her father's death in 1543 culminated with the
experience of the "ecce homo." Together with the call she felt
in reading the *Confessions*, Teresa describes this as her second
conversion that takes place in the Lent of 1554, when Teresa
was thirty-nine years old. (Teresa calls this her second
conversion, baptism being the first. Some commentators refer
to it as her third conversion, after baptism and religious vows).
Certainly, 1554 is a critical date in Teresa's life, separating the
ascetical period of her life from the mystical. Teresa calls the
part before 1554 "her life," and the part after "the life God lived
in her."

Teresa and the Reform of the Order of Mt. Carmel (See *Autobiography*, chapters 32-36)

In the meantime, Teresa's spiritual life became deeper
and richer. At the same time she lacked appropriate and
knowledgeable spiritual direction and became concerned
about the authentic nature of her spiritual encounters with the

Lord—a natural reaction given the presence in Spain at the time of several women whose religious experiences were considered illusionary. She went to see Fr. Gaspar Daza, a diocesan priest of Avila and Don Francisco de Salcedo, a layman (See *Autobiography*, chapter 23). The meeting was the start of a new phase in Teresa's life that led to her writing her autobiography (1562, 1565), the *Way of Perfection* (1566), and the *Interior Castle* (1577). In these years Teresa's spiritual life moved through the first mystical graces (1554-1562), a period of ecstasy (1562-1572), and finally to perfect union (1572-1582).

From around 1558 Teresa began thinking of setting up a reformed house within the Order of Mt. Carmel. Until this time all Carmelite convents and monasteries lived according to the 1432 "Bull of Mitigation." In 1559 she had discussions with Peter of Alcántara which probably included such an idea of reform, since Peter was involved in similar Franciscan reforms (L. 32.13). At this time, Teresa was forty-five years old and reasonably happy at the Incarnation. However, she had several visions that included commands to start the work of reform (L. 32.11). As these ideas became known, Teresa experienced lots of opposition, especially within the Incarnation (L. 32.14; 35.2). This lasted about five to six months, during which time Teresa was withdrawn and no longer had the confirming visions. However, behind the scenes Teresa began to collect money, and her sister Doña Juana de Ahumada and her husband Don Juan de Ovalle bought a small property. Teresa gained further support from some wealthy ladies, including Doña Luisa de la Cerda, with whom Teresa was spending a six month stay following the death of the lady's husband. However, Teresa wanted the new convent to be without endowment in imitation of the original Carmelite rule; an idea supported by Peter of Alcántara. Teresa had wanted very much to found the community in poverty and had defended this idea strongly (L. 35.1-7), but towards the end of her life she had to reconcile herself to its impracticability in some cases as she indicated in one of her letters to Father Gracían in February of 1581.

> When we read that Teresa wished to return to the primitive observance, it does not mean returning to the original rule as given to the monks on Mount Carmel by Albert, Patriarch of Jerusalem. In the case of the Carmelites, first nuns and then friars, reform meant going back to the primitive observance and laying aside all the dispensations granted by popes from Eugene IV (1432) onward, and partly as a result of problems caused by decline, the Hundred Years War, schism, abuses in the mendicant orders, and the Black Death. The mitigations were considered a softening of the original vocation, and reform demanded they be laid aside. When Teresa began the reform, it essentially meant a return to simplicity, authenticity of religious life, austerity, poverty, deeper silence, and solitude to allow for contemplation.

Teresa returned to the Incarnation in 1562 for the election of a new prioress (L. 35.7), and awaiting her was Peter of Alcántara, together with the Bishop of Avila, who presented Teresa with a brief and permission from Rome for a new convent (L. 36.1). On August 24th 1562, the feast of St Bartholomew, Teresa established the first foundation of the Reform, St. Joseph's. However, from August 1562 until August 1564 dispute arose among the various authorities which led to a law suit before the Royal Council (L. 36.17). In 1563 Teresa was given provisional permission and went with her first companions to the new convent. Later, official permission was confirmed but not finalized until 1567.

The fifteenth and sixteenth centuries were times of religious reform in Spain. Several religious communities undertook a return to the more primitive observance of their rules. Mother Teresa began her reform around 1562 when she founded the first house for her community in Avila.

On April 11th 1567, the Carmelite general, Fr. Rubeo, arrived in Avila from Rome. Although Teresa was anxious he might oppose the Reform, he instead was very supportive and gave permissions for more foundations. In fact, in August he sent authorization for two Reform foundations for men. Teresa's second foundation was in Medina del Campo, set up without endowments. Two nuns from St. Joseph's together with four nuns from the Incarnation, including the sub-prioress, along with a young girl who was able to pay the rent for the building until they were settled in, became the community for the second foundation. Teresa also moved ahead with her desire to include Carmelite friars in the Reform and established the first house in Duruelo with the commitment of John of the Cross and Antonio de Heredia. Within two years Teresa had made other foundations for women in Malagón, Valladolid, Toledo, and a second for men in Pastrana.

From 1570-1575 Teresa expanded her foundations from Salamanca to Seville, including Alba de Tormes (where Teresa is buried), Segovia, Beas de Segura, Granada, and Caravaca. However, in October 1571 Teresa was appointed prioress of the great convent of the Incarnation. It was an unusual appointment—not an election—since Teresa was from the Reform and the Incarnation was not. This led to lots of problems and divisiveness. One of Teresa's first decisions was to nominate John of the Cross as confessor for the community, and the two of them were able to quickly establish peace and renewal. In 1576 Teresa continued her foundation work, setting up convents in Villanueva, Palencia, Soria, and Burgos, along with a monastery for men in Alcalá. In July 1577 Teresa returned to Avila and remained there for two years. She then made her final journey to visit her communities.

Contemporary challenges of Teresa of Avila

1. Teresa is a real saint, who lived through the ups and downs of life, who struggled with yearnings for spiritual growth while getting bogged down in the typical failures of weak human beings. May she be a model for us in our own longings to grow and to be rid of our failures.
2. There is no genuine leadership until the leader has followers who believe in what the leader believes in. Let us pray that Teresa will touch a chord in our lives and lead us to give ourselves to God.
3. Teresa died in 1582, was beatified in 1614, and canonized in 1622. She was declared the first woman doctor of the Church in 1970. Her life is considered an open book for us to follow. May we learn from her life and values.

Chapter Two

Teresa the mystic

"Mother Teresa of Jesus is regarding the things of this world a very great woman, and as regards the things of the next greater still" (Padre Pablo Hernandez, S.J., contemporary of Teresa). There is no doubt we are concerned with a really great person—a great woman, a great saint, a great universal teacher. The only way for us today to know Teresa is through her writings approached with knowledge and understanding. We need to get to know the woman, her background, training, life, and forming environment, so that we can get to know the saint. Then we need to know both woman and saint to understand her writings and make them life for us and profit from them. We have already considered the major steps in her life and turn now to look at the development of her spiritual life.

Stages in the development of Teresa's spiritual life

In her writings Teresa communicates a personal interior experience and not the traditional revealed theological notions of the Church. The scope of her work was not specifically doctrinal but practical, apostolic, and vital. This does not mean that Teresa does not convey the faith of the Church. She does! That is the whole point of studying her spiritual life. She is not just communicating knowledge, but life. So, it is important for us to know the stages in Teresa's spiritual life. Our understanding of Teresa's life and experience is the point of departure for us to later understand the doctrine contained in her life experience. Her experience and teaching authority are directly connected and we cannot understand the latter without the former. Teresa was born in 1515 and died at the age of 67 in 1582. Some people can write books on prayer because they have studied it, but Teresa wrote only from personal experience.

In Avila Teresa is known as "la Santa." No one denies she was a dynamic and powerful woman who knew all the great people of her day, including the king. Nor do they overlook the fact that she was an outstanding business woman who developed a huge multifaceted community in a man's world. But she was essentially for people of her day, as she is for us, "la Santa." She teaches us by the fact that she encountered God and can help us in our search. Her spiritual life was divided into two great parts by the important fact of what she called her third conversion in 1554 (baptism, vows, and 1554).[1] Prior to 1554 was the ascetical part of her life and can be viewed in three periods; period of childhood (1515-1531), period of vocation (1532-1543), and period of pre-mystical experience (1544-1554). Already in her childhood Teresa evidenced a love for God and religious values. Between six to ten years old Teresa and her brother, Rodrigo, tried in their own way to give themselves to prayer, and later they planned to leave by night to go in search of martyrdom among the Moors of southern Spain. However, these early signs of religious devotion met with obstacles as Teresa fell into typical adolescent crises of vanity, worldliness, attachments, and frivolous readings. This became so disturbing to her father that he decided to send her to a boarding school nearby in the hope that the nuns in the monastery of St. Mary of Grace might be able to help Teresa regain some seriousness and religious devotion.

Ascetical life. When we think of asceticism today we often understand the terms to refer to the rigorous practices of self-denial that we find in almost every religious tradition, practices that include the abstinence from all worldly pleasures to pursue a higher spiritual goal. However, the original term in Greek simply referred to exercise or training—so some kind of active preparation for the pursuit of improvement in certain aspects of life. Taking the stages of spiritual life presented by Teresa of Avila—which most Christian spiritual writers use today, ascetical life refers to those stages in which a person is actively involved in preparing himself or herself for spiritual development and especially for union with God in contemplation. Asceticism is active, and contemplation is passive; asceticism is what we do, contemplation is what God does in us. Teresa calls the first "my life," and the second "the life that God lives in me."

The second period in the ascetical phase of her life, the period of vocation, began around 1532 with visits to her Uncle Pedro de Cepeda who introduced her to spiritual readings, and also with visits to her sister's house where she spent time in reflecting on her own future in light of an increasing awareness of hell. This led Teresa to seek entrance into the Carmelite Monastery of the Incarnation in Avila, to profession two years later, and to a time of peace and satisfaction in religious life. There followed a serious illness which Teresa was able to accept with patience and at the same time to maintain an intense spiritual life. At this time Teresa deepened her life of prayer, reaching the prayer of quiet and even of union. So, she arrived at the threshold of the mystical life and received the first grace of infused prayer. But as with the period of childhood, a new crisis arose, due this time to community tepidity, lack of real interest on the part of her confessor, no knowledgeable spiritual director, and social, society type friendships. Added to all of this, and perhaps a deeper reason for her crisis, was a false humility that led Teresa to give up prayer entirely for almost a year, in 1543.

The third period in Teresa's ascetical phase of life began in 1544; this was the pre-mystical period of her life. It was a slow and difficult comeback that started with her father's death. Teresa began to take up spiritual direction and to recommit herself to prayer. She made efforts against her negative tendencies, attachments, and comfortable life, and all this led to a general state of aridity and dryness which lasted ten years. She finally arrived at her third conversion in 1554.

So, this ascetical period of her life had three parts, each about 11-12 years. The ascetical period lacked continuity, rather we see three ups and downs. Each time she arrived at the threshold of contemplation and mystical life and then fell back, due to a typical adolescent crisis in 1531 and to superficial community weaknesses in 1543. It is particularly interesting as we consider the contemporary significance of Teresa of Avila that her comeback and eventual conversion parallels the movement of reform in the Council of Trent in 1544-1545.

1554 was the date of Teresa's major conversion and total dedication to contemplative and mystical life, and there followed three periods of mystical prayer; 1554-62, the first mystical graces and early union; 1562-72 a period of ecstasy; and 1572-82 total union. There was no crisis in this period rather stability and continuity characterized the whole period from 1554 until her death. For Teresa there were no alternating plateaus and nights as in John of the Cross. Rather, for Teresa purification and growth went hand in hand. The period of the first mystical graces began with the first forms of infused contemplation, recollection and a sense of the presence of God. Teresa found that it was no longer necessary to represent Christ or God. She experienced that God was always there with her but that it was now possible to sense God's presence. There were three components to this new stage: recollection and interiorization, contemplation and the inability to meditate, and infusion—an intervention of a new dynamism within her that was greater than all her previous efforts. This period, with its extraordinary experiences of the humanity of Christ (L. 27.3; 28.1, 4), was not without severe sickness, trials, doubts, and temptations (L. 30.8; 31.1).

Mystical life refers to that part of the spiritual journey in which a person is passive. The original term "mysticism" came from a Greek word meaning to close, or to hide, or to conceal. So, in spirituality mystical life is that part of life that seems secret, or hidden, or inaccessible to the normal disciple of a religious tradition. The only way to gain access to the mystical life is by opening oneself to passively receive enlightenment as a gift from God. In Teresa's stages in life and prayer, the mystical life refers to contemplation, the prayer of quiet ("quiete" in Latin means "at rest," so passive, receptive), ecstatic prayer, and the prayer of union. These stages are ones in which the disciple is not active, but passive, open, and receptive to God's actions.

The second period in Teresa's mystical phase of life was the ecstatic period which included a flood of extraordinary graces. These unusual graces came after visions and revelations and were elevations of the spirit within and beyond simple union. At times they manifested the violence that this new life placed on the whole person of Teresa, and her struggles to adapt to this new style of God-directed life. This period culminated with the mystical experiences linked to her entrance into the sixth mansion. Teresa describes many of these in the final chapters of her *Autobiography*.

The third and final period in the mystical phase of Teresa's life consisted in the experience of consummated union, and with it the state of peace, and even confirmation in grace. This was a time of absence of ecstatic and mystical graces. Rather, she had a continual experience of an intellectual vision of the Holy Trinity. This period corresponded with the seventh mansion and also with Teresa's most intense apostolic activity.

What was the content of Teresa's spiritual experience?

We say that Teresa's spiritual life is a source of guidance for us in appreciating the nature of life with God in general. We are accustomed to studying Scripture, Church teaching, the conclusions of theologians, and so on, to understand the nature of spiritual life. In Teresa's case we say that she, too, is a source of knowledge for us. But to show the relationship between the life of Teresa and her teaching we need to highlight the content, in fact, the dogmatic content, of her spiritual experience. This means dealing with the problem of whether someone's personal experience, in this case Teresa's, can be a universal teacher. And we will leave this kind of discussion for the next chapter.

Spirituality consists in men's and women's grace-filled efforts to become who they are capable of being. Since God is always drawing us to divine life, human efforts are not so much attempts to move forward and grow, but rather they are attempts to cut false values that keep us from God, to thwart our own resistance to God's grace. Each life is a vocation to become more than we already are—personally, socially, cosmically, and wholistically. Sin is the thwarting of this growth potential by refusing to be more than we are now, to be for others in love, to be with others in community. Spirituality, then, is letting our life develop in the love-filled atmosphere of God's grace, where we grow naturally and effortlessly, provided we remove all hindrances to growth. "The Christian of the future will be a mystic or he or she will not exist at all. . . . by mysticism we mean . . . a genuine experience of God emerging from the very heart of our existence.[2] To become a mystic is the most important calling of our lives, and Teresa is the great model for all of us.

Human beings are not psychologically aware of the supernatural; so we cannot distinguish between an act of theological charity and philanthropy. But in the case of some mystics, besides the possession of supernatural reality they also have the added ability to experience it, even though this experience is never full, since an element of faith always remains. When mystics experience God's presence they do so dynamically and vitally, integrating dogmatic content and an experience of it. Regarding Teresa's spiritual and mystical experiences we want to know what she experiences (the dogmatic content) and how she experiences it (the psychological content).

So, let us first look at a series of objects that form the content of Teresa of Avila's mystical experience. She experienced herself—as an image of God, as capable of grace, as transformed by the supernatural, and as home of the divinity. It is not that Teresa believed this, rather, she experienced it. Teresa had experiences of Christ in a progressive way—an intellectual experience of Christ, an experience of Christ's humanity, an experience of Christ as the source of grace, an experience of Christ in the Eucharist, and an experience of the glorified Christ. Teresa also gained a progressive experience of the presence of God—from an external appreciation of the universal presence of God in everything, to an appreciation of the internal presence of God in the inner spirit of each of us, to an experience of the indwelling of the Trinity, present in each of us and in the whole of creation. Teresa experienced the Word of God, especially the biblical Word of God, as spiritually efficacious and as producing a sanctifying effect within her. Teresa also experienced the Church, in fact she had a twofold direct experience of the ecclesial mystery; she experienced the earthly reality of the Church and she experienced the heavenly reality of the Church. Teresa also has the direct experience of the mystery of evil, of sin, and of hell. Finally, Teresa experienced the mystery of grace. This experience was vast, from the plan of salvation, to the mediation of Christ, to the efficacy of interior grace. It progressed to the relationship between grace and sin, between grace and the development of the spiritual life, and to the efficacy of mystical graces.

When we look at the content of Teresa's experience, it is like reading a book of theology, or reciting the creed. It is not only the content of Teresa's experience, it is also the content of our faith. In looking at the "what" of her experience, we can also immediately see the "how." In each case, God led Teresa to a deeper experience of each element from more exterior aspects to more interior ones. Put another way, Teresa's experience was the pursuit of God into the very depth of her own being. In yet another way, we can say that Teresa was progressively immersed in the mystery of God. This process of an ever deeper awareness and experience of God was linked in Teresa's life with a series of mystical phenomena.

The relationship between Teresa's spiritual experiences and her teachings

Teresa's teaching depends on her experience. She has no other source. So, as her experience developed so too did her teaching. So, there was a chronological link between her experience and the composition of each of her writings. Teresa's mystical life lasted about twenty-eight to thirty years, being progressively enriched throughout that time. Her later writings are based on deeper experiences and so contain more extensive teachings than her earlier ones. Prior to 1554 Teresa was in the ascetical period of her life, with its struggles and its ups and downs. Teresa wrote nothing at that time. Beginning in 1544 Teresa went through what we can call mystical initiation, with some sporadic special experiences granted by God. In 1554 she entered a crisis due to the conversional experience she had that led her to seek advice from confessors and counselors. They asked her to write out a general confession of her sins with some mention of the graces she thought she was having. She found it difficult to express herself in such unusual topics and simply underlined appropriate references in a book of devotion. In 1559 Teresa met Peter of Alcántara who assured her that her experiences were genuine. This gave Teresa a sense of freedom and confidence and from then on she was able to express herself with clarity. She wrote her first spiritual testimony in 1560. She was then in the fifth mansion, the life of union, and wrote the first edition of the *Life* in 1562. A little later, when already in the sixth mansion, the life of ecstasy, she wrote the second edition of the *Life* in 1565, with its extraordinary exposition of the four stages of prayer (Chapters 11-22). During this same period (1562-72) Teresa wrote the *Way of Perfection* with its detailed exposition on preparations and method of prayer. In 1572 Teresa entered the final stage of the spiritual life, the seventh mansion, and in 1577 she wrote the masterpiece, *The Interior Castle*, which is one of the greatest presentations on prayer in the entire history of spirituality. In 1581 Teresa wrote her last spiritual testimony regarding her own spiritual life.

Thus, glancing at the relationship between her spiritual experiences and her teachings, we can see that the last stages of the mystical life are not treated in her earlier works because she has not yet experienced them. So, her teachings on prayer are incomplete in the *Life*—she has only four stages that cover four to five of the mansions. The teachings on prayer in the *Interior Castle* are complete and mature, described in seven stages, because she has now experienced them all. It is worth noting that with the progression of mystical experience comes for Teresa a charism of communication. At first she could not explain what she had experienced, and simply underlined sections in a book. Later, after her meeting with Peter of Alcántara she was fully conscious of her experiences and had an ability to explain them to others. As time passed Teresa was able to modify earlier ideas, even correct some thought, as her experiences progressed and she gained greater clarity.

Major convictions that guided and motivated Teresa

The stages that we see in studying Teresa's spiritual life happen to her from God's love. She does not plan or program these developments. Rather, Teresa lives motivated by a series of fundamental convictions that guided her life. We cannot imitate Teresa's stages of prayer in our spiritual lives, but we can foster in our lives her convictions. Scholars refer to Teresa's "ideario espiritual," a collection of ideas or motivating convictions regarding the spiritual life. These spiritual convictions can also motivate our lives. Let us have a look at some of the major convictions that led Teresa in her life and can do so for us too.

1. Human condition. There is a level of life beyond this one that gives meaning to this one. So, we live with an awareness of the supernatural in life. We live in the here and now in light of the there and then.
2. Life with God. Struggles are a normal part of the spiritual life. However, we are able to face struggles because we are immersed in the love and mercy of God. We can never view one without the other.
3. Spiritual life. This is God's gift to us, but we must contribute too. Spiritual life needs determination and fortitude.
4. Preparations for prayer. We need a remote, adequate preparation consisting in a life of virtue and the practice and method of prayer. Too many people leave these out. We must contribute basic good living and three essential virtues—charity, detachment, and humility (love, integrated living, and realism).
5. A central idea—recollection that includes focused attention and appreciation of God's presence. This means a simple "method" of centering attention, appreciating that God is very close, being fully present to the beauty of each moment.
6. Our call and vocation. Spiritual life is love, friendship, and union.
7. Our response as Church. Teresa stresses the ecclesial and sanctifying value of prayer. We often think ministry is our contribution, and prayer nourishes ministry. Perhaps the opposite is more correct.

8. A new vision of reality. We must contemplate God everywhere, in everything, in us, and in our world.
9. A key suggestion for those who wish to follow Teresa. You must have a decisive, heroic effort never to abandon the life of prayer.

These are the major convictions that motivated Teresa's life. As she lived them with dedication, God called her and gifted her with spiritual growth beyond anything she had anticipated. We cannot pursue the stages of growth in prayer and life, for they are gifts from God. However, we can dedicate ourselves to make these convictions our own, leaving to God the growth that sometimes follows.

Contemporary challenges of Teresa of Avila

1. Teresa of Avila went through two decades of spiritual mediocrity. Teresa's early life evidenced dedication, but her goodness and dedication went astray. This often happens to us too. In spiritual life we must understand all that we have and all that we might lose.
2. Our lives can be full of cares, concerns, and worries, either inherent in life or self-inflicted. This was so with Teresa. A tragic spiritual sickness we often face is that we become deluded into thinking our spirituality is effective. We need peace to examine our lives and discover the direction we must take.
3. If we are not growing spiritually we are standing still, while people around us may well be surging ahead. The fault for

lack of spiritual growth is in ourselves. We expect something or someone to save us when no one else can, except ourselves.

Chapter Three

Teresa the writer and teacher

Teresa of Avila had little formal education and yet her writings are now considered masterpieces in the history of spirituality. Teresa's three major works may well contain many grammatical, formal, and stylistic mistakes or defects, but it is hard to put them down if you want to learn about the stages in the spiritual life and in the life of prayer. Soon the reader feels Teresa is talking to him or her, and experiences being welcomed into an intimate circle of friends who share the common goal of seeking deeper union with God in love through prayer. In this chapter we seek to learn more about Teresa as a writer and teacher.

Teresa as a writer

Teresa's works are among the greatest spiritual writings of world history, and in our own generation, we continue to encounter Teresa in her writings. Sometimes we find ourselves confused by the way she speaks about herself and presents her teachings—at one minute she tells us to pay attention to her advice and the next she tells us she is the worst person in the world! We need to understand the characteristics of her writing so that we can appreciate her advice, the doctrinal content of her works, and prepare for an eventual interpretation of them. Teresa's writings are not systematic, nor scientific. Rather, they are very personal and so a little exceptional. She often passes from a personal experience to claim that her teachings are of a universal value. Her writings were originally intended for her contemplative sisters who had little theological training, and she wrote to offer them practical advice about their spiritual lives and especially the life of prayer. In her writings she sees all spiritual experience in light of the mystical experience, and this must be kept in mind by all who read her works. At the same time her writings are also destined for a group of theologians who review them, often in view of the new teachings of the Council of Trent. These theologians who are confessors, guides, and analysts change from being judges to being disciples as their interaction with Teresa and her writings progresses.

Apart from her letters, poems, and some of her spiritual testimonies, all of which Teresa wrote spontaneously and with interest, her major works were all written under obedience to her confessors or to the provincial. Teresa evidenced resistance to these demands, partly because at times she believed she had better use for her time and partly because of the psychological resistance she felt to writing about spiritual matters while being a woman and illiterate in a world where only men studied and then specialized in theology. Moreover, Teresa's reluctance was also due to the delicacy of the themes and the attitudes of the Spanish Inquisition in those times. So, Teresa wrote her work from beginning to end without any division, and when she left off writing to go to sing the Office or perform other duties she never re-read her work upon returning—she clearly thought it was a waste of time! (L. 30.22; see also 14.8). Teresa did not organize or think things through before writing and generally did not bother to correct or touch up her work when she finished—although that changed later in interaction with the reviewers of her work. Of course this characteristic of immediacy produces a very positive value in her works, namely their characteristic of testimony or direct witness. Only when she had finished, did Teresa divide up her text, give titles to the chapters, and then, in some cases, a final title to the book.

Teresa is a writer that we must get to know if we want to understand our own or other people's spiritual life and growth. All Christian approaches to prayer today are dependent on the life, experience, teachings, and interpretations of Teresa of Avila.

The Spanish inquisition was originally the work of the Catholic Monarchs (1479), and was charged with seeking out heretics and finding Jews and Muslims who covertly continued to practice their faiths. The first grand inquisitor in Spain was Tomas de Torquemada (1420-98), a fanatic who put to death more than 2,000 people. Eventually, the control over the Inquisition passed to Philip II. The intolerance of the Inquisition was directed also to Catholics, including the archbishop of Toledo, Bartolomé Carranza, the famous scholar, Luis de León, the great saint and reformer, John of Avila, and Ignatius of Loyola. These famous individuals and lots of ordinary people were persecuted by a few who maintained a rigorous interpretation of what they considered orthodoxy.

Teresa's preparation as a writer

Teresa's ability as a writer was very limited. She showed no knowledge of capital letters, used very little punctuation—for example she never used a question mark or an exclamation mark—and in general was ignorant of grammar. Moreover, she wrote rapidly, adding to the confusion. One author calls Teresa's writing "a sweet disorder" (gracioso disorden).[3] When Luis de León was asked to review Teresa's work for the Spanish Inquisition, he listed some of her weakness as a writer: "incessant ellipses; confused grammatical agreements, enormous parentheses, which cause the reader to lose the train of thought; lines of reasoning that are never completed because of interruptions; verb less sentences."[4]

We must remember that Teresa had no specific preparation as a writer. She learned to read and write, first at home and then at the monastery of Our Lady of Grace. But she would have had no preparation in the task of composing anything. She read the lives of the saints and lots of novels, and maybe as a child she tried to write a short story. Her preparation to write on spiritual matters was weak. While as a young woman she had the elementary formation suitable for a housewife in those days, her religious formation still had many gaps in it. We know that after her religious profession, Teresa read several spiritual books. Her uncle Don Pedro de Cepeda gave her the *Letters of St. Jerome,* and when she was sick she read the *Commentary on Job* by Pope Gregory the Great. When she was around forty years old she read the *Confessions* of St. Augustine, and a book on prayer and meditation by Luis of Granada. Her Uncle, Don Pedro, gave her a book which she found very helpful; *The Ascent of Mount Sion,* by Bernadino of Laredo. When asked to write down the sins and graces of her life, and being unable to articulate the graces, she underlined sections from *The Third Spiritual Alphabet* by Francis of Osuna. However, in all these cases we would have to acknowledge that while some of them made a great impact on Teresa when she read them, they had no influence on her formation as a writer.

It seems clear that Teresa lacked any real preparation as a writer. She had done some spiritual reading, benefitted from speaking to her confessors and theologians, and knew some holy people and their lives and experiences. However, when she wrote she did so spontaneously and never consulted books for topics under consideration. This meant that she had no doctrinal preconceptions. She simply wrote about things that she had personally experienced. Moreover, when she wrote, her works were conversational—she was simply talking to her readers, as she still is today. Throughout her works her intentions were strictly practical—she was teaching her nuns and giving them lots of practical advice. When she gave descriptions they were psychological rather than abstract analysis. However, Teresa was and is a charismatic writer who created a spiritual climate for her readers and continues to do so for us today.

> *The major writings of Teresa of Avila*
>
> *1560 First Spiritual Testimony*
> *1562 First edition of the Autobiography*
> *1565 Definitive edition of the Autobiography*
> *1566 Way of Perfection*
> *1573 Foundations*
> *1577 Interior Castle*

The religious environment in which Teresa lived and wrote

Martin Luther, a young German Augustinian friar, posted his ninety-five theses on the door of the castle church of Wittenberg on October 31 1517, just over two years after Teresa's birth. Initially, his challenge was against the selling of indulgences, but eventually it became a rejection of the medieval view of Church, sacraments, and more. There were many abuses within the Roman Church at the time, and there was a clear need for a renewal and reform. Eventually, Paul III (1534-49), under pressure from Charles V, called the Council of Trent in 1545 to deal with the challenges facing the Church. The Council's teaching would be of particular interest throughout Teresa's life, and many of the changes to Teresa's writings, especially her autobiography, were demanded by censors because of Trent's teachings. At a deeper level, the reform of Trent would have a parallel in the spiritual reform of Carmel. The final phase of spiritual renewal leading to Teresa's great conversion of 1554 paralleled the preparations and build up to the Council of Trent. The culminating points of Trent had correspondence with a new direction in Carmelite reform, the ecclesiastical reforms following Trent found parallels in the reforms initiated by Teresa, and as the leaders of Trent become reformers, so too did Teresa.

The Council's main document was that on justification, which insisted that a person is totally transformed by God's justification and not merely externally considered justified as Luther had stated. In the former, grace removes sin, but the latter is a radical denial of the interior supernatural order. Teresa's vivid experiences of God's transforming actions within her became embodiments of Trent's teaching and at the same time real living challenges to Luther's mere external assignment of justice.

The fifteenth and sixteenth centuries were times of religious reform throughout Europe, and especially in Spain, where Philip II was anxious to be seen as a leader in the reforms demanded by the Council of Trent. As part of this movement, Mother Teresa began her reform around 1562 when she founded the first house for her community in Avila. She had suffered for many years in her own mediocre religious life, in the need of conversion and spiritual renewal, and from incompetent spiritual directors. She insisted that both her nuns and friars in her reform be knowledgeable of religious issues. She gave a good theological foundation to the spiritual renewal of her communities, and she wrote extensively for the formation of the nuns. Teresa was not a trained theologian, but her works were reviewed by outstanding scholars. She also simplified the Divine Office and insisted that it be formative for the nuns, especially in their knowledge of Scripture, and so should be read in the vernacular. So, the renewal and reform that Teresa initiated was part of the enthusiasm of the times, but well-grounded theologically, biblically, and spiritually.

Above all, reform was a daily necessity, as it is in the life of all reflective people. Whether you wear sandals and socks (Calced) or not (Discalced) is a not an issue. What is relevant is whether your heart is totally given to God in love.

> We have the originals of nearly all Teresa's principal works, thanks to Philip II's desire for original manuscripts for his library at El Escorial. Unfortunately among the many copies are several with errors. However, in 1586 the General Chapter of the Discalced Carmelites entrusted the editorship of Teresa's complete works to none other than Fr. Luis de León. His work was published in Salamanca in 1588, but it excludes the Foundations. Further editions came quickly, some with errors and additions, so in 1661 a new official edition was produced, a collaborative effort under the direction of P. Francisco de Santa Maria. In 1881 there was yet another edition, unfortunately again with errors. In 1915-24 P. Silverio de Santa Teresa produced the definitive edition which is the basis for most contemporary translations.

The means that Teresa uses when writing

As we have seen, Teresa was very spontaneous in her writing. She did not have any doctrinal system, and consequently no doctrinal preconceptions. She had a series of spiritual convictions that motivated her life. These convictions were practical not abstract. So, regarding the doctrinal content, Teresa did not use any particular means, but she did have several ways she used to express her convictions. She utilized several approaches to express the content of her convictions and several that aided in cultivating a general spirit in appreciating what she presented.

So, when we look at Teresa today we find that she uses images and comparisons although both are used for pedagogical reasons and not for literary ones. She uses them to express what otherwise is ineffable. Unlike John of the Cross, Teresa rarely uses symbols and metaphors. She does use allegories, often to serve a structural purpose in her work, although at times the distinction between allegories and comparisons is not clear. In fact, some of her great treatises and syntheses, notably the *Interior Castle*, are built around allegories. Most of the allegories that Teresa uses are taken directly from nature and daily life. She speaks of water and fountains, running water and stagnant water, a well, river, rain, sea, clouds, and morning mist—each giving clarity to her presentations of spiritual matters. She also speaks of the sea and a sponge, a drop of water and the entire ocean. On other occasions Teresa speaks about a flame and fire, a fire-arrow, a fire and the heart, and she takes these ideas further and speaks of the sun and a candle. At times she talks about the dawn and dusk, a diamond and crystal, and even of a castle of diamond. She makes excellent use of the distinction between a mirror and a reflection, or a person and a portrait, or a crucible and gold. Teresa likes the images of birds, an eagle, a phoenix, a dove and a dovecote, or bees, a bee-hive, and honey. She finds a lot to say about spiritual life when she thinks of the life of a silkworm until it becomes a butterfly. Coming from Avila with its reputation for military leadership, Teresa speaks of chess, battles, a standard bearer, soldiers and the king, a castle, and war. Then again Teresa can use well the contrast between a giant and straw, an emperor and a beggar, a theologian and a shepherd. On other occasions she utilizes the image of a baby that suckles, or marriage symbols, and then also other biblical images. Teresa's preferences are water, fire, castle, and the affective life. She especially uses allegories for major doctrinal themes such as the interior life, the life of prayer, mystical graces, and the presence of God.

At times Teresa uses aids to help in creating a general spirit for what she wants to convey. After all she is trying to communicate a vital experience, and this is not achieved by content and doctrine, but by creating a spirit that catches the reader up in the experience. Teresa succeeds beautifully in establishing a close relationship between herself and the reader. She uses invocations, exclamations, monologues with God, and doxologies or prayer, and the reader is allowed to listen in and share these intimate moments (L. 16.8). At times, Teresa engages in a dialogue with the reader and each one is invited to respond. In some sections of her writings she relives past experiences, sometimes intense affective experiences, at other times sentiments or horror at sin and personal failure. On other occasions she expresses a strong sense of the transcendence of God. In and through all of these Teresa conveys a charism of mystical awareness as she transfers the reader to a supernatural level.

Teresa the teacher

When we immerse ourselves in the works of Teresa of Avila we must confront two important questions. First, what value can we give to a particular, individual spiritual magisterium in the Church? With Teresa we are not dealing with a school of spirituality, even though one does arise from her teachings. Rather, we are asking whether there can be authoritative teaching based on one person. We do have examples of individuals who became authoritative teachers and interpreters but generally their work was and is in Scripture or doctrine, or morals, but not spirituality. Secondly, we ask what is the value of a magisterium based on personal experiences and not on a theological synthesis of many. Put another way these two questions confront the issue of the ecclesial value of saints and sanctity.

One of the principal objections to this teaching authority of Teresa is the fact that her teachings are too linked to her own personality and are therefore very particular, subjective, and dependent on her own psychological state. They are not objective nor are they based directly on Scripture or liturgy. So we need to ask whether a message which begins from a personal experience can become of universal value. Teresa does not receive revelations for the Church, as do Bridget of Sweden or Catherine of Siena. There is always the distinction between a universal economy of salvation and a particular one for each of us. That is true, but we are not talking about that here. Rather, we are asking if a particular experience or insight into spirituality can become universally valid for all of us.

No individual or group can ever satisfy everyone or exhaust the universal message. That is why we have many spiritualities in the Church. There are always common elements because all spiritualities must be based on revelation. The Second Vatican Council dealt with the Word of God and the means to transmit it (*Dogmatic Constitution on Revelation*, #8) and identified three sources for the authentic transmission and interpretation of the sources of faith: the magisterium of the Church, theological reflection, and charismatic life. Teresa is part of this last group and we study her not because she is part of the hierarchy or a part of a school of theology, but only because she is a saint. Sanctity is the work of grace, and saints are in and for the Church, always gifts to specific times and needs of the Church. After all we encounter the fullness of the Church in its living members and not in doctrine. Each period in the Church's history has its own saints, grace-filled individuals who live out the message and challenge of the Church, fulfilling a specific task given them by God.

Teresa is a saint given to the Church in the sixteenth century. Her final ascent to spiritual maturity and union with God parallels the early work of the Council of Trent. When the Council began, so too did Teresa's pre-mystical stage of life. The culminating point of the Council's teaching was the triumph of the mystical life in the document on justification. The implementation of the Council's challenges corresponded with Teresa's work of reform. So, Teresa is a reformer like Trent—however, one of many. Teresa's specific response that is unique to her is that she is the embodiment of supernatural life and of justification through internal grace, a reply to the merely external assignment of forgiveness. Teresa is a reply to Luther's arguments because of her vivid experience of the interior supernatural life.

The source of Teresa's magisterium is interior experience and not revealed theological notions, her doctrinal contribution is not scientific but descriptive, not speculative and doctrinal but practical and apostolic, not a communication of knowledge but a communication of life. Of course many people do this in one way or another and can inspire their friends and acquaintances. In Teresa's case, over time, people throughout the Church have felt she expresses what they understand their calling to be. In other words, Teresa has gained a certain canonical status in the Church. She is a teacher for all of us and her teaching on spirituality is authoritative.

A few conclusions to keep in mind when reading Teresa's works

When reading Teresa's works we must always keep in mind the characteristics and limitations of her writings and teachings. Her writings are not systematic and theological, but practical and pedagogical. We should also stress the importance of the relationship between Teresa and the reader. Teresa's writings are direct and spontaneous, and they do not follow a scheme but provide a dialogue between her and her reader. So, readers should not bother too much about the details of the text but rather enter into the general spirit, for Teresa is more interested in communicating rather than informing. It is always good to just listen to Teresa rather than read her. We should also remember that there is a hierarchy of spiritual values to be obtained from her works. First we must come to grips with the person and her life. Then enter the spiritual atmosphere that permeates her works. Third, we should identify the primary convictions that motivate her in all that she does—identify her "ideario espiritual." Finally, we should see the picture of the spiritual life and its development and respond to her challenges.

Contemporary challenges of Teresa of Avila

1. Teresa does not offer us a methodological guide to the spiritual life. Sometimes there are too many layers to our spiritual lives. Often detailed facts and organized advice are not as important as a spirit and a feeling that lead us to truth. Teresa creates a spiritual environment that can enthuse us and challenge us. May we open our hearts to receive the challenges the Lord has for us.

2. Teresa's audience for her major works was both the sisters who yearned for her teachings and a group of theologians who were anxious to protect her and her teachings—along with themselves—from criticisms by the Inquisition. Today's inquisitions, too, will want to criticize and degrade contemporary dedication to spiritual life and its challenges, and we must have the courage and fortitude to continue in faith.

3. The spiritual convictions that motivated Teresa's spiritual life are the critical analytical components of her life as far as we can appreciate them. What are the spiritual convictions that motivate our lives today—and what should they be?

Chapter Four

The *Autobiography* of St. Teresa of Avila

W e call Teresa's first work her *Autobiography* or her *Life*, even though it is not a biography as we understand such books today. Sure, there are references to her life that help us reconstruct basic facts about her family (1515-1535), her time in the convent of the Incarnation (1535-1562), and the final years when she starts the reform at St. Josephs (1562-1565). However, beyond these helpful facts, the *Autobiography* deals primarily with Teresa's interior life leading up to 1554 and her third conversion and then describes the graces she receives from God after 1554 up to 1565. The *Autobiography* of St. Teresa of Avila is a truly wonderful book, one of the great masterpieces of Christian spirituality, and it offers great spiritual benefit to readers.

Some difficulties we can encounter in reading this wonderful book

The *Autobiography* is a very personal book that deals with the intimate aspects of Teresa's spiritual life, with both her struggles and her extraordinary graces. To reap the benefits of its teachings, to gain from the inspiration that it offers on every page, and to be enthused by its challenging vision of a life of prayer, we must read this book well aware of its complicated origin and very special characteristics. Moreover, we must read it with awareness of Teresa's own life development and especially her spiritual experiences—both of which we have seen in previous chapters. The *Autobiography* is a heterogeneous book, first written as a sort of general confession and so marked with a definite penitential aspect, but as time passes and the readers immerse themselves in Teresa's deep spiritual transformation, it becomes eminently doctrinal and didactic. So, it begins as a confession and ends as one of the greatest teachings on prayer in Christian history. However, we are faced with this constant dualism which is its originality, and our awareness of this is the key to our understanding the book.

> Commenting on the Autobiography, E. Allison Peers says, "I find in it—as every reader must—innate talent of a very high order: vividness of description, flexibility of expression, a captivating freshness, an earnestness and a devotion which in their moments of greater intensity are irresistible."[5]

As a result of its dualist focus—confession and doctrine—the *Autobiography* is a reserved book, a semi-secret writing. Written as a sacramental confession in view of spiritual direction and at the same time written as a personal self-denunciation to offset the possible inroads of the Inquisition. However, it eventually takes on an authoritative presentation on mysticism and prayer—a magisterial focus that permeates the book. In the title to chapter ten Teresa is clearly the teacher who is in charge of the content of her presentation and even instructs the readers to keep secret what she is writing about. In fact, she later tells her reader that he may publish material about her failings but that she refuses permission for any divulgation of the graces she has experienced (L. 10.7). As a further aspect of the semi-secret nature of this book, Teresa often writes in an intimate and confidential way to one or other of the recipients of her work, which gives an enigmatic dimension to the book. She describes her failures and graces freely, gives and withdraws permission regarding who may read or not read her work, tells one to destroy her work if it is inappropriate, and reminds readers of promises they have made (L. 10.8). At times she feels confident in entrusting readers with her most personal interactions with God, and then tells them to tear up what she has just written (L. 16.8). While submitting her work to the readers she actually calls one of them her son and tells him that since he claims to love her he must prove it by preparing himself for deeper union with God (L. 16.6). So, as the history of the text develops it is clear that the material can only be understood by those who are already on the mystical way.

In reading the *Autobiography*, one quickly sees that Teresa is well aware of the atmosphere in Spain in the years following the Council of Trent and in the oppressive times of the Inquisition, so she leaves her book with a definite anonymity. She never mentions any of her convents and never gives anyone's name—except Peter of Alcántara, who was already dead, and Francis Borgia, who was no longer in the country. So, no one can be implicated in any position that the Inquisition may find objectionable. When Teresa finished her book, the readers took it away before she had time to re-read or correct it, and she barely had time to add a note asking that the whole manuscript be re-written so that no one would even recognize her writing (L. Epilogue, 2).

So, the *Autobiography* contains the first attempts of Teresa of Avila to draw from her personal experiences teachings of universal value regarding the spiritual life and prayer. This is done in two stages: first, testimony about her life, sins, and graces, and second, interpretation and explanation of her life experience as it benefits others. These two stages correspond to the two editions of the *Autobiography* in 1562 and 1565.

Origin of the *Autobiography* of St. Teresa of Avila

In 1554, Teresa experienced a crisis of conscience after her first experiences of mystical graces following her conversion. The worrying question was whether these graces were genuine or illusions, and this concern was all the more relevant given the existence in Spain of several women whose mysticism was judged to be false. Teresa consulted two advisors and they demanded a written account of her sins and graces, with emphasis on the former since that is where they believed the problem would lie. Teresa wrote down her sins and failings but was unable to describe the ineffable graces (L. 12.6). So, she underlined the relevant parts in a book by Bernadino of Laredo, *The Ascent of Mount Sion* (L. 23.12). This is about 1555. Teresa pointed out to her readers that it is one thing to have these experiences and quite another one to explain them to others (L. 17.5). The two initial reviewers of Teresa's work were Fr. Gaspar Daza and Don Francisco de Salcedo, and their judgment was that Teresa's experiences were false and the result of evil, and they further suggested that Teresa should consult with a learned Jesuit priest (L. 23.14). So, Teresa submitted her experiences to the Jesuit but her inability to express herself remained (L. 12.6). This continued until 1559 when Peter of Alcántara came on the scene and removed Teresa's anxiety by confirming that he knew from personal experience that Teresa's graces were authentic (L. 30. 2, 4). Shortly after meeting Peter of Alcántara, Teresa could confidently express herself with extraordinary clarity, so much so that she appeared to have received the double charism of understanding and expressing her spiritual experiences. There followed in 1560 her first *Spiritual Testimony* concerning her initial mystical graces. In January 1562, Teresa went to Toledo and stayed there for six months, finishing the first edition of the *Autobiography* in June 1562. So, Teresa finished the first edition of the *Autobiography* three years after the publication of the "Index of Forbidden Books."

Once her spiritual directors read these new communications they began to realize what they were dealing with, and instead of being judges they became disciples of Teresa. They asked Teresa to rewrite her work emphasizing her graces and only referring to the sins in passing (L. 30.22; 37.1). She then claimed that besides answering the directors' questions she also wanted to attract others to the service of

God and to a deeper experience of prayer (L. 18.8). Teresa evidenced a sense of her own authority (L. Epilogue, 2). She explained in detail the graces the Lord has granted her and as soon as she had finished the text the readers and "censors" who had become disciples (L. 16.6), take it from her (L. Epilogue, 2). This was in 1565. This is the actual text of the *Autobiography* that we presently have. Teresa calls her autobiography the "big book" and both the *Way of Perfection* and the *Interior Castle* are to be understood in light of the *Autobiography*.

So, the *Autobiography* was written in two different spiritual situations; where narrative and teaching meet. The first spiritual climate was crisis, penitential, confession, written for directors as confessors. The second spiritual situation was one of security, where the confessional decreases and the teaching increases, written for directors and confessors who had become disciples. Put another way, there are three tempos to the *Autobiography*: historical-confessional, personal-interior life, and interpretation-teaching.

Some external influences on the composition of Teresa's *Autobiography*

We have seen that the *Autobiography* was written under two influences—the mystical life of Teresa and the various pressures of her confessors and directors. The interaction of these two influences profoundly affected the content and structure of the book. So, it helps us to understand the book better when we know something about the external circumstances that influenced the composition of the book, to know who the recipients of this work were, and to appreciate what was the inner state of mind of Teresa as she wrote this important work.

We need to repeat yet again because of its importance that the proximate reason for writing the book was the crisis of conscience that Teresa felt because of her experiences of her first mystical graces. At that critical time Teresa had no suitable spiritual director who had the appropriate skill and ability to evaluate what was happening to her (L. 23.2). To some extent the lack of availability of directors, or their unwillingness to get involved, was due also to fear of the possible interventions of the Inquisition, at a time when it was already involved in many cases of pseudo-mystics, most of whom were women. Even when Teresa found a Jesuit who was willing and competent she was aware that people told him to avoid her, so much so that she felt she would end up with no one who would hear her confession or give her guidance (L. 28.14; 29.4). Moreover, when it became known that Teresa had unusual spiritual experiences friends came to warn her that she could get into serious trouble with the Inquisition (L. 33.5). Opposition from all sides took its toll, and Teresa felt besieged, especially by good people, and this left her overwhelmed and discouraged (L. 28.18). This was a situation that lasted about five to six years, 1555-1561.

The interventions of the Inquisition were always hanging over the heads of all concerned with the Autobiography. Teresa had several friends who were suspected of links to Illuminism and were brought before the Inquisition. The Autobiography was mentioned in one of the Inquisition's investigations and the reviewer demanded a copy immediately. Many people sought to read the "Life," and while access was carefully guarded, a former friend of Teresa denounced it to the Inquisition. Fortunately the Inquisition appointed Fr. Domingo Bañéz as censor, and he approved it. However, the manuscript was not returned until after Teresa's death.

A second significant influence on the composition of Teresa's *Autobiography* was the interaction with the recipients of her writing. This group of readers was in constant dialogue with her and she often speaks to one or other of them in a confidential way (L. 16.6, 8). We know three of them with certainty: the Dominican priest, García de Toledo who is the principal recipient of the work, a diocesan priest from Avila, Gaspare Daza, and a layman, Francisco de Salcedo. Two others are probably involved: the Jesuit priest, Baldassaro Alva, and the famous Dominican theologian, Domingo Báñez. There are also three others who had important influences on Teresa's reflections at this time: the Dominican, Peter Ibáñez, the Franciscan, St. Peter of Alcántara, and the Jesuit, St. Francis Borgia (L. 24.3). All these formed a spiritual group around Teresa, and while some of them started with little interest, some opposition, and mediocrity in their own spiritual commitment, they all gradually participated in the mystical graces themselves. So, the *Autobiography* was written in an environment of intense mystical fervor for people some of whom were themselves beginners in mystical life. They formed a company of intimate friends, and Teresa referred to them as "the five of us who at present love each other in Christ," and urged them to form a secret pact, pledged to encourage each other in spiritual growth (L. 16.7). When Teresa wrote, she stuck to her primary task of personal revelation, but often digressed to encourage readers and to give them advice in their own mystical development (L. 16.6; 17.5). So, once again we see how the work serves a double function, self-revelation and testimony on the one hand and lessons and teaching on the other. Teresa transformed what was supposed to be a confession and a self-denunciation for judgment into a presentation of self-defense, authoritative teaching, and guidance for others.

A third influence on the writing of the *Autobiography* was Teresa's own inner state as she wrote. This, after all, was the immediate context for the book. She wrote with absolute sincerity and, after 1559 and the double charism of communication, she wrote with full awareness of the charismatic value of her words and experiences (L. 17.5). In the second half of 1560, Teresa began the contemplative experience of the humanity of Christ, visions in which she saw with the eyes of her soul that Jesus was beside her (L. 27.2). This became "a new book" for her, taking the place of spiritual books in the vernacular recently withdrawn by the Inquisition (L. 26.5). There followed three years of uninterrupted mystical experiences of the humanity of Christ (L. 29.2). Then other mystical graces followed up to the writing of the *Autobiography*, new graces on an affective level that included increases in the love of God in her, impulses of love, with one she describes as the piercing of her heart with an arrow of love from God (L. 29.2, 8; see also 20.9-13). It is in this state that Teresa writes the *Autobiography* (L. 20.13).

So, the *Autobiography* has a complex origin with two editions (1562 and 1565), changes in the attitudes of the recipients, and development in the mystical life of Teresa. All these developments lead us to understand the dualism and heterogeneous nature of this great work. The *Autobiography* is historical and narrative in the first edition and doctrinal and mystical in the final text; the first edition is strictly reserved, the final edition is accessible to everyone.

The structure of the *Autobiography*

There are four parts to the *Autobiography*.

1. (Chps. 1-10) This is historical, a narrative of external facts. It belongs to the first edition and describes the preliminaries of Teresa's mystical life.
2. (Chps. 11-22) This is a digression, a mini treatise on prayer. It is a doctrinal explanation of the stages in prayer growth that Teresa had experienced up to this time. It is a doctrinal elaboration of the second edition, a codification and interpretation of the stages in the development of the life of prayer.
3. (Chps 23-31) This is a fusion of historical facts and doctrinal explanations. It narrates the interior spiritual experiences of Teresa after her third conversion and after each section gives a doctrinal evaluation. This part picks up from where Teresa left off at the end of chapter 10.
4. (Chps. 32-40). This is completely from the second edition since all the facts are after 1562. It integrates external events, interior experiences, and doctrinal interpretations. It opens to considerations of the mystical life in the militant Church (chps 32-36 describe some foundations) and to the Church triumphant (chps 37-40 describe supreme mystical graces that are pre-beatific).

At first, the *Autobiography* may seem disordered but this is due to its origin and to the two editions. We are dealing with a life that becomes teaching for us, and so a form of lived doctrine. Besides the structural outline as we now have it, we should also keep in mind the organic synthesis of the work.

1. This first part deals with Teresa's call almost to the mystical life, along with her resistance, sin, fights, and final divine triumph.

2. As she writes about the initial mystical graces, she pauses to think about how far she has come since those times and makes a parenthesis to describe what has happened to her in the last few years. This becomes a mini-treatise on prayer and how God watered her arid soul in four distinct ways.

3. Teresa then returns to where she left off at the end of chapter ten and describes events after her conversion of 1554. Her spiritual life becomes an immensely Trinitarian life, a foretaste of future union. This interior fullness leads to the final part.

4. This section describes the great apostolic work of Teresa in the foundations.

Teresa's teachings on prayer in the *Autobiography* (including a summary of chapters 11-22)

The *Autobiography* is a specially qualified spiritual witness by Teresa, a synthesis of the whole evolution of the spiritual life as she had experienced it up to the writing of the *Autobiography*. Throughout, she seems particularly concerned with beginners in the spiritual life and establishes a dialogue with them, sharing her own imperfections, taking time to explain the early stages in detail, and urges them on in spite of difficulties and trials in the beginning of their efforts. Throughout the book she weaves four key concepts. The first is her emphasis on the presence of the supernatural and the interior transformation that God effects in the soul. The second emphasis that weaves its way throughout the text is Teresa's experience of the mercy of God—Teresa had actually wanted to call this writing "A book of the mercies of God." The third emphasis, the central theme of the book, is Teresa's teachings on prayer not as an exercise but as a way of life. The fourth emphasis is the efficacy of mystical graces for both personal and ecclesial growth. Perhaps the most helpful teaching is that contained in chapters 11-22 where Teresa digresses to present four stages in the life of prayer.

> Teresa "gives expression to her ideas in images picked at random from the world that she sees around her. Grace is a shining river, sin a sluggish pool. A bad habit is as hard to uproot as a plant that having been watered every day has grown so strong that it has to be dug out with a spade. A soul full of eager desire is like a fountain spurting up from the earth; a soul in rapture like vapor drawn heavenward by the sun. A soul that has not recourse to God moves at the pace of a hen. . . Someone at the mercy of a stupid director is as frustrated as a tethered gosling. Those who live by prayer are as safe as the spectators who watch a bullfight from the grandstand."[6]

Prior to her conversion in 1554, Teresa had endured ten years of dryness in her spiritual life. This general state of aridity had weighed heavily on her, and it is no surprise that when a renewed dedication to prayer comes she sees it as water that refreshes dry, parched land (L. 4.9). Teresa also loved to think of herself as a garden in which the Lord took a pleasant walk (L. 14.9). When she mentions her third conversion she is immediately carried away with enthusiasm regarding how the Lord blessed her in prayer following that conversion, and she describes four stages in this grace-filled period as four ways in which the Lord watered her dried-up spirit. The first way is to draw water from a well which is a lot of work. The second way is to use a water-wheel and a canal or aqueduct. This is easier than the first way but it is still laborious for you have to keep turning the water-wheel. The third way is to redirect the flow of a river or stream. This is better than the other two although now and again dirt can fall into the stream and block the flow. The fourth way is when the garden is watered by a constant rain. This is the best and requires the least effort. These four ways of watering the garden of the soul correspond to four degrees of prayer.

First water—Meditative Prayer (L. 11-13). Once a person becomes determined to give himself or herself to God in love, to become a servant of love, and to seek out perfect love, then he or she resolutely pursues the path of prayer. This will require humility, courageous perseverance, and constant effort at the beginning. The first degree of prayer corresponds to the stage of beginners, they who must work hard in trying to be recollected, to avoid distractions, and to repent of past failings. This is a period of vocal prayer or meditation. God helps at every stage, but this is an active phase and a person must contribute a lot to persevere in times of dryness. This first stage is discursive meditation. It is hard work and seems to have few rewards, but it is a time when the Lord trains and tests a person who seeks union in love. It is the beginning of mental prayer and one must approach it with determination, humility, and fortitude of soul, and do this amidst all life's distractions without desire for consolations.

There is a lot a person can do to help himself or herself in this first stage. One can make necessary efforts to facilitate recollection, detachment, and solitude. One can reflect on one's past, recall the presence of God, do what one knows pleases God, and increase self-knowledge. One can use one's imagination to focus on thoughts of God, to make acts to awaken love, to formulate resolutions to help one's dedication, to speak with Christ to affirm his continued presence. It is also valuable to be content where one is without yearning for spiritual graces that are beyond one at this early stage.

A person who seeks God in prayer will find there are many temptations to confront, even in this early stage. One should not be overanxious about possibly losing the little one has gained. One must live in the real world with all its distractions. Even healthy recreation can have a recuperative effect. One should have confidence that God is drawing a person to spiritual growth. So, one should not lose confidence, but walk with courage and a genuine humility that appreciates the personal call of God to growth in the spiritual life. One should avoid becoming stingy-hearted, maintain great desires, and seek solitude and silence. Then, one must avoid laziness, backsliding, neglect of one's duties, fear, and judging others' worthiness. This first stage of prayer is discursive reflection, but one must avoid excessive intellectual exercises and reasoning. Throughout this first stage when one finds it necessary one should seek counsel from prudent, experienced, and knowledgeable spiritual directors.

Second water—the Prayer of Quiet (L. 14-15). The second way of bringing water to the garden of the soul is by using a waterwheel and an aqueduct. Cranking the waterwheel puts water in the canal and it then flows to the garden. It is not necessary to crank the wheel all the time, so there is less effort and work at this stage. "Quiete" in Latin means "at rest" and here refers to an initial passivity—the will is passive but not the faculties of intellect and memory. Teresa thinks of turning the crank of the waterwheel as the constant working of the intellect. The will is occupied in God alone—a person wants nothing except to love God. The will is captivated by an intimate awareness of God's presence in the depths of one's being. The intellect and memory can help the will focus on God's love, thinking about and remembering love, although at other times they can be distracting. However, at this stage a person should try not be distracted by the faculties, otherwise he or she will quench the spark of love.

With God's continued help this stage leads to growth in virtues and to a clear focus on God, with the resulting decrease of interest in all that does not lead to God. This is a delightful anticipation of the stages of union that lie ahead. It is also a time of growing awareness that God understands us, wants to be present to us, and longs to lead us to transformation. A problem that arises at this time is that one who is in it often does not understand what is happening, especially in times of dryness in prayer. This is a time of purification and a challenge to humility. So, it is important one cultivate humility and avoid deliberately seeking consolations.

The recollection that one experiences along with peace is very satisfying and many who reach this stage think it is the end and do not pass beyond it. But this is a first stage of recollection, a little spark of the love of God, in which the will is united to God even when the other faculties are distracted. It is a period of special gift and must be nurtured by the avoidance of sin and by a commitment never to abandon prayer. One must understand this love and appreciate it is only a beginning and continue to prepare oneself for what lies ahead. One must control the distractions of the intellect and memory, as if accumulation of thoughts, ideas, and even good memories can maintain this spark of love! One should not smother the flame with ideas, reflections, memories, applications, theological formulations of prayers. All the reason has to do is understand that there is no reason. One cannot force this situation or earn God's love, but can help by making non-discursive acts of love and commitment, and quietly place oneself with simplicity in God's presence. At this time one enjoys a quiet that God gives and is not something we earn.

So, the prayer of quiet is beyond the hard work of meditation and is a first stage in contemplation. While infused contemplation is a new way of knowing and so affects the intellect, the prayer of quiet transforms the will so that it focuses on God alone. It is a time of profound peace and recollection nurtured by silence and simplicity. At this time, the will focuses on God alone, and the other faculties, although still active and at times distracting, become more focused on God. The prayer of quiet is a time when one is aware that God is present, communicating something of divine life. At first it can be sporadic but can eventually become frequent and habitual.

Third water—the Prayer of the Sleep of the Faculties (L. 16-17). One of the easiest ways to water a garden is when you have a small river nearby that you can divert. Then there is very little work involved except having to keep the channel clear. In this stage of prayer there is so little work that God takes over and is now the gardener. This is the prayer of the sleep of the faculties when the faculties only have the ability to be occupied completely with God and have no interest in anything else. This passive, mystical experience is God's work within a person and results in an initial union of one's entire being with God. It is a painful experience since it includes a death to all earthly interests, but it is a delightful immersion in the love of God. While one retains the realization of being in this world and the body shares in the delights of the soul, a person and all his or her faculties are totally centered on God even though they can still function, in fact can still be engaged in business matters or works of charity. However, a person seems taken over by God and while faculties continue to function that is not where their interest lies. This stage is not totally passive; the faculties can understand what God is doing in them. A person wants exclusively to be with God. Teresa describes how in this prayer she seems frozen in place, beside herself in a delightful disquiet. The only possible response at this time is complete abandonment of oneself into God's hands—for one no longer feels he or she belongs to self anymore. God is now the gardener and achieves un-thought of growth in a person's life—in virtues, in humility, in fortitude, and in wisdom. So, a person can abandon himself or herself to God and to whatever God wishes to achieve in him or her.

This prayer is similar to the prayer of quiet, except that the latter is focused on the passivity of the will alone. In fact, Teresa says she appreciated this is not complete union yet it is deeper than the prayer of quiet, but says she did not at first see any difference. The former leads to a holy idleness in God, whereas in this stage the whole person is immersed and focused on God while his or her faculties can continue to function in normal daily activity. Teresa says Mary is an example of the former whereas Mary and Martha together exemplify the latter. The former is initial contemplation; the latter is a union of both active and contemplative lives. In the prayer of the sleep of the faculties a person is in union with God in a life beyond this one while still living in the here and now. A person knows he or she is different but does not know how or why. There is now an inner dynamism greater than all previous experiences. Still living in the here and now, one's entire being lives elsewhere.

Fourth water—Prayer of Simple Union (L. 18-21). When Teresa writes the second edition of her *Autobiography* (1565), she is in the sixth mansion (1562-72), so when she describes the fourth water as the prayer of simple union, she is referring to the union she has experienced up to that point. In 1572 she enters the final stage of the spiritual life and describes that experience when she writes the *Interior Castle* in 1577. This fourth stage of prayer is an extraordinary prayerful experience of the complete passivity of all the faculties and their total union with God. The rains are pouring down and soaking and saturating the garden with no effort on the part of the gardener. While producing the most overwhelming enjoyment and delight, a person cannot express the joy he or she experiences, since no power or feeling remains in the senses or faculties—they are totally dead to all that is not God. There is no effort in this prayer for it is all gift—a profound union and elevation of the spirit which God gives, as and when God wishes. Teresa says that when it happens she feels taken out of herself, carried away in a swoon, wondering if it is a dream, as she becomes unconnected to this world. She says she experiences a suspension of all her faculties and a total absence of sensory consciousness, so that at the time she feels nothing and understands nothing although afterwards she is aware that something extraordinary has happened to her. The total suspension of all faculties lasts only a short time and then either intellect or memory returns. Over a period of time the intellect and memory can go in and out of this suspension. This prayer and union produce extraordinary transformation in a person and progress in virtues. He or she experiences growth in courage and determination, in humility and self-knowledge, in awareness of God's love and compassion, and in an increased dedication to the service of others.

In the prayer of this fourth stage the soul experiences profound union with God in the depths of one's inner spirit. Accompanying this prayerful union and identification of the soul with God there arises stronger experiences of ecstasy that affect the person interiorly and exteriorly. It seems God is carrying off the body as well as the soul. Within the experience of union God lifts up the soul to witness the gifts God has prepared. At this time a person feels taken out of his or her body, leaving it seemingly lifeless. One can see this is happening and can do nothing about it, but must have courage to let go and let God be in control. When this elevation is strong a person cannot resist and can even lose control over his or her body. Teresa speaks of times of ecstasy and levitations she experienced.

These experiences of ecstasy manifest the awesome power of God and can cause fear in the recipient, although this fear is accompanied by gratitude and love. Ecstasy also produces a different experience of detachment of the body and abandonment of this world's values. It leads to an intense desire to serve and to an understanding that God gives all the necessary strength. It is also a time of purification and pain. In times of ecstasy the soul is transformed in God and gains extraordinary renewal of life, and then all it does is in conformity with God's will.

Following ecstasy and intense experiences of union a person can find himself or herself immersed in profound pain that touches the depths of one's spirit. This experience comes after the visions and revelations. It is a pain of intense desire, felt in solitude. God's communications do not console but intensify the pain of an extreme sense of solitude, aloneness, and abandonment in the desert. In love with God alone, nothing else satisfies, all is centered on God. So much so that as all the faculties' functions were suspended and centered on God in the prayer of union, so now they are all suspended and centered on the pain of this anxious longing and love. So one can long for death to gain the union that alone removes the pain, and yet there is a joy in the pain for it is the crazy pain of love that purifies for greater love. Teresa writes the final edition of the *Autobiography* while she is in the midst of these experiences. Teresa says the soul is ready to risk its life to get away from the great illusion in which we live and to be in the real life of union with God in love.

A person now wants to do everything to be of service to God and to do all according to God's will. Entirely focused on God alone, everything about this world now wearies him or her. A person goes around in a fog, feeling in exile, having no interest in this world, and longing for the next. The union of this fourth stage of prayer, together with the elevations of ecstasy are God's gifts, and a person in this stage knows this in the depths of his or her being. This produces boldness, humility, purification, perfect commitment, and a sense of wonder at the greatness of God's works within one's total life experience.

Teresa concludes her section on the four waters with a reflection on the importance of focusing our thoughts and prayers on the humanity of Christ. She warns against raising the spirit to high imageless contemplation too soon and suggests we leave that to God. She stresses that our own humanity requires union with the humanity of Christ (L. 22:10). She says she sees some who lack humility in appreciating their own creatureliness and its need of support in the humanity of Christ. Even for those who seek imageless union she points out that the image of Jesus is not like other corporeal images. True enough, she acknowledges, the prayer of union includes the suspension of all senses and faculties, however, we still need to keep the humanity of Christ ever before us for we are human and need human supports.

A few final thoughts from Teresa

- When you give yourself to a life of prayer you are learning to be a servant of love.
- Your life of prayer becomes more and more an intimate sharing between friends.
- Take time frequently to be alone with God who loves you. May your love endure and may you pursue God's will in everything.
- See everything through the lens of love; keep divine love always before your eyes.
- Remember that lovers see the world differently, and you will too. Remember love always begets more love.

- You are not just called to prayer but to growth in prayer.
- Never be afraid, take courage, set out with determination on the path of deeper spiritual life

Chapter Five

The Way of Perfection

Teresa gave the final version of the *Autobiography* to the readers in 1565. The nuns of the monastery of St Joseph's heard about it but were not allowed to read it because Fr. Báñez, OP., opposed its publication and the Spanish Inquisition banned all spiritual books in the vernacular. Following the insistence of the nuns, Teresa offered to write a little book that would achieve two things. First, it would be a book on religious life and the acquisition of virtue to help the nuns in their spiritual lives, but Teresa modifies this idea so that it becomes a book on the practice of prayer and the life of prayer. Second, it would be a preparation for them to eventually read the *Autobiography* if and when permission was given for its distribution.

The origin of the *Way of Perfection*

The *Way of Perfection* is St. Teresa of Avila's principal ascetical work. It is not a book that is intended to offer testimony about her own spiritual life; rather it is strictly pedagogical. She intended it to be an aid to teaching the nuns about the life and values of the Order of Our Lady of Mount Carmel. Teresa referred to the book as her advice and counsel to her nuns. Later, others gave it the title *Way of Perfection* and Teresa accepted it. It is written in the style of a long letter to her nuns with no pre-determined plan or system. The recipients were twelve nuns of the first monastery of the Reform that Teresa had opened in Avila, dedicated to St. Joseph. Therefore, it is very specifically characterized—it is for those twelve nuns. It is simply intended as a sort of initiation to religious life according to the spirit of Carmel. St. Joseph's had just been founded and consisted of a small group of nuns who had lots of fervor for their new life and were in the first stages of the mystical life.

Although Teresa had intended this as a very simple aid to the nuns, it actually became Teresa's most elaborate writing. She worked on it for about sixteen years, almost to her death. It is the only work she personally allowed to be sent to the printers, but she died before it was published. This work has a long and painful history which influenced both its final composition and its doctrinal content. Moreover, it would seem that some of the nuns wanted guidance on the later stages of the spiritual life while others had more basic needs, and Teresa tried to respond to their varied needs.

Teresa wrote this book at great speed but it turned out to have a complicated editing or redactional history, passing through several versions due to the readers' concerns over the newly published teachings of the Council of Trent and the inquisitorial atmosphere in Spain at the time. Teresa finished the final version around 1566 but kept revising it right up to her death. She actually authorized its publication in Portugal in 1579-81 (even then the Portuguese Inquisition took our chapter 31 on the prayer of quiet).

Teresa wanted the Way of Perfection to be read and published. It was her gift to her sisters. "Thus, we can assume how important it was for her to pass on to her sisters the wisdom and practice contained in this book. It was to be her legacy to them, containing the essence of her life as a way of formation in the Lord."[7]

History of the *Way of Perfection*

The *Way of Perfection* went through five stages in its development. The nuns of St. Joseph's had heard about the *Life* but could not read it partly because it was so personal, even confessional, and also because Fr. Báñez opposed its publication and diffusion. Moreover, in 1559 the Inquisition prohibited spiritual works and the future writing of that sort of work. Teresa agreed to write something as a simple introduction to prayer which would in turn prepare the nuns to eventually read and appreciate the *Life* if and when that became possible. In the meantime, Fr. Báñez gave Teresa permission to write something on prayer for her sisters (W. Prologue.1). Teresa wrote the *Way* at great speed. Her first intention was very simple, namely to give advice on religious life and the practice of the rule and constitution of the Order. Although she also says that where appropriate she will add elements from the *Autobiography* (W. Prologue. 4). She then modified this to include teachings on prayer that can lead to a life of prayer. To fulfill the second intention she digressed again to comment on the "Our Father" and "Hail Mary," but her comments on the "Our Father" became so long that she omitted the "Hail Mary."

In dealing with the subject of prayer, Teresa does not succeed or possibly does not choose to avoid topics considered dangerous and suspect by the Inquisition. So, in places the work becomes polemical, ironic, and vivacious. Some of the topics Teresa deals with that were considered polemical in her day were the value of vocal prayer and its relationship to mental prayer, the dangers of a "life of prayer," the apostolic value of contemplative life, the attitude of women and nuns in leading a contemplative life, the sufficiency or not of merely vocal prayer—including the material recitation of the divine office by nuns, and the suitability of reading spiritual books in one's own language. Teresa had to know that these were "unacceptable topics," and yet she still addressed them! This was done when the atmosphere in Spain at the time included humanism, pseudo-mysticism, and illuminism, when genuine spiritual people and rigid orthodox theologians were often in conflict, when the primate of Spain was imprisoned by the Inquisition (1559), and when the writings of leading figures like John of Avila and Francis Borgia were put on the "Index of Forbidden Books." It was precisely at this time that Teresa wrote some fiery pages and dealt with many of the topics under discussion by the great figures of the day. She had no chance of getting the approval of the Inquisition and this was now necessary even for the distribution of manuscripts. She first sent the work to Fr. Domingo Báñez, her confessor at the time, but for some unknown reason he never saw the work, which might be as well, since there was little likelihood that he would have approved it. She then sent it to Fr. García de Toledo who became the primary reviewer. All this was in the first half of 1566.

The second phase in the book's history began with the review by Fr. García de Toledo. He did not approve of the work, partly because of its polemical tone, partly because of fear of the Inquisition, and partly because of the prohibition on spiritual books and manuscripts. In his reply to Teresa Fr. García de Toledo spoke about "theological imprecisions," "incorrect statements of doctrine," and "unsuitable style." He felt the book was too polemical, ironic, and familiar. He went on to censure several themes in the book: certain biblical interpretations, Teresa's desire for death, the fear of quietism in the prayer of quiet, and comments on our merits before God and their relationship to the recently published documents of the Council of Trent.

Fr. García's review led to a third stage in the history of the *Way*, namely Teresa's second edition of the *Way*. Fr. García was a very close friend of Teresa and his negative evaluation led Teresa to re-write the entire work. She not only corrected where indicated but changed and developed a lot of material on literary and doctrinal levels. On a literary level she decreased the polemical aspects of the work, made it anonymous, canceled spontaneous mystical effusions, and made it less intimate. On a doctrinal level she elaborated on the love of God, on liberty of conscience in the choice of confessors, on the careful selection of religious vocations, and on the necessity and efficacy of mental prayer. While she changed a lot, she still stuck to some of her criticisms in the first writing but phrased them differently. All this took place probably in 1566. In fact, as a spiritual book the second edition became more balanced, calm, and accessible to all.

A fourth stage in the history of the book followed with a series of new censures by the theologians who read it. This new text was submitted to at least three censors, Fr. García and two others. Fr. García and an unknown second reader, who is now referred to as Pseudo-Báñez since for some time it was thought to be Fr. Báñez, imposed a further series of doctrinal corrections. Most of these corrections referred to material in the documents of the Council of Trent: the nature of pure love, the desire for death, justification, and the relationship between infused contemplation and the state of sin.

The corrections by Fr. García and others led to the final revision of the book by Teresa. She accepted the corrections, and continued revision of all the manuscripts distributed to her convents right up to her death. Sometime around 1579-81 the Portuguese archbishop of Evora asked Teresa's permission to print the work and Teresa agreed. However, the Portuguese Inquisition suppressed chapter thirty-one on the prayer of quiet.

Structure of the *Way of Perfection*

When Teresa started the *Way of Perfection* she did not have any clearly formulated outline or structure. In fact, she says that she does not know what she is going to say and doubts she will say it in an orderly way (W. Prologue. 2). In spite of all the changes to the *Way of Perfection*, it still has a good unity and structure. Teresa's basic purpose still remains, to offer to her nuns in St. Joseph's some practical advice for contemplative life according to the spirit of Carmel. Its primitive doctrinal nucleus also remains, as does the basic pedagogical form with which Teresa started her project. It is a preparation for mystical life and for an eventual reading of the *Life* if that ever becomes possible. Teresa presents her teachings in two stages. First she emphasizes a radical preparation for the mystical life which consists in the practice of virtue. She then follows this with an immediate preparation for the mystical life which consists in the practices of prayer. These two stages give rise to the two parts of the book. Part one is the fundamental ascetical part consisting of chosen virtues as foundation for the mystical life of prayer. Part two deals with the internal ascetical life of prayer itself. To these two parts Teresa adds an introduction on the apostolic value of contemplative life.

So, we now have the general outline of the book:

Introduction (chps. 1-3). The purpose of contemplative life

Part I (chps. 4-15). The practice of virtues basic to contemplative life

Part II (chps. 16-42). Prayer

- Prayer in general (chps. 16-26). A theoretical presentation on the life of prayer
- A practical pedagogical section. A concrete way of developing prayer based on the "Our Father" (chps. 27-42)

Teachings and doctrinal content of the *Way of Perfection*

The *Way of Perfection* by Teresa of Avila is not a systematic presentation but a practical one. Nevertheless, it is based on two or three fundamental convictions or theses. First, in the introduction, it stresses the ecclesial and sanctifying value of the life of prayer. Interestingly enough, Philip II had just sent a circular to all contemplative communities imposing prayer for the success of the Council of Trent. Second, Teresa also teaches the absolute necessity of an adequate preparation for the life of prayer. This preparation is dealt with in part one and emphasizes the ascetical dedication consisting in the practice of virtues. In this context, Teresa stresses detachment, humility, charity, and fortitude. Third thesis in Teresa's teaching is the need of a gradual and well organized practice of prayer. Teresa presents these three basic theses of the book directly in her teachings and indirectly with the aid of images, symbols, and allegories. She uses many literary devices as we have seen in the *Autobiography*. In this book her principal ones are way, water, master, interior palace, war, and chess. She uses "way" as the journey to God and claims to present the best one which is also a short cut, namely prayer. When she uses water, she distinguishes between stagnant and flowing as early and later stages in prayer.

In the *Way of Perfection* Teresa presents four major doctrinal points. The first one she addresses is the relationship between prayer and spiritual life. She insists that prayer is not to be seen as a practice of piety—as it frequently was in her day, but rather as a complete way of developing one's spiritual life. Understood in this way prayer has great sanctifying and apostolic value. Teresa also deals with the relationship between the practice of virtues and the development of the life of prayer. Second, as we have seen, she underlines three important virtues, love, detachment, and humility. Teresa sees these three virtues as the foundation for the life of prayer, for they free a person to give himself or herself to God. She urges her sisters that they practice these three virtues with fortitude, what she calls "una determinada determinación." If one practices these virtues with the totality of one's self-gift then these three virtues become pure-love, total detachment, and humility-truth. However, in the pursuit of these three virtues one must always remember that any growth is God's gift and not the result of our efforts.

The third doctrinal point that she discusses is the relationship between mystical contemplation and perfection. This is a theoretical question and basically deals with whether a sinner can reach mystical contemplation. Since she wishes to preserve God's sovereign will to do whatever God wishes, her answer is "yes," but generally such a person does not reach contemplation because one normally needs the practice of virtues. However, she goes on to comment that not all who practice virtues arrive at contemplation. So, holiness is possible without contemplation. However, again she stresses that contemplation is a short-cut to holiness and perfection. Teresa prefers to speak of union rather than perfection, and thus she avoids subjectivism. How does a person gain access to this short-cut? By following the *Way of Perfection*.

Teresa's final doctrinal point is her teaching on the interior asceticism of prayer. Prayer must be a total way of life, a progressive movement to union with another person in love. While there is no fixed method there are certain basic elements that a dedicated individual should pursue. Before all else a person should respond to the basic demand to make a decisive, heroic effort never to abandon the life of prayer. Then one should dedicate himself or herself to the three forms of prayer, vocal—provided it is not just material or a mindless babble of words, but includes reflection, mental discursive prayer—meditation, and simple interior prayer—recollection which can become the beginning of contemplation. It is important to Teresa that we stress that every form of prayer must include recollection for this can prepare us to think, speak, listen, and receive.

Teresa's teaching on prayer in the *Way of Perfection*

One of the reasons why Teresa chose to write the *Way of Perfection* was to satisfy her sisters' requests for guidance in their religious life and in prayer. They could not read the *Autobiography* but were hopeful that Teresa could still help them in view of her own experiences in prayer. In the *Way of Perfection* she gives a solid theoretical presentation of prayer along with lots of practical advice and counsel.

Teresa gave her sisters a good foundation in knowledge about the spiritual life and the life of prayer. She wrote to one of the superiors, Fr. Mariano de San Benito, "If you want us to serve you well in these houses of ours, my Father, send us women of intelligence, and you will see that we shall not be in the least worried about their dowries." To a prioress who complained about a nun who read a lot, Teresa replied, "Better a bookworm than a fool."

Foundations for a life of prayer. Teresa gives three qualities that are foundational for anyone who wishes to follow the way of prayer, qualities that are basic to all human, Christian development. These qualities bring the peace of soul needed for advancement in prayer. They are first, love for one another; two, detachment from all created things; and three, true humility, which is the main quality and must permeate the other two. These three fundamental attitudes consist in a just relationship to oneself—not based on attachment to things, a just relationship to others—not in possessing others but in an authentic love, and a just relationship to God—not in pride but in authentic humility. These three attitudes are transformed by hope, love, and faith and reflect the three evangelical counsels of poverty, chastity, and obedience to God's will.

Love (Way of Perfection chaps. 4-7). Love for one another is essential for all spiritual growth. It must not be weakened by excessive particular, preferential loves that can destroy authentic community by focusing on some to the neglect of others. The love that Teresa recommends is a universal spiritual love, it is a new way of viewing the world, seeing all from the perspective of love. Teresa says that those to whom God reveals this vision of the world love differently than those who have not received this communication (W. 6.3). A person with this love is without self-interest, seeks and rejoices in the good of others, and is always ready to suffer for others and their good. This love includes compassion, patience, and sensitivity to others' needs. Although this love is selfless and focused on God alone, it does not exclude passion and intensity in one's love of God and of others.

Detachment (*Way of Perfection* chps. 8-14). Detachment from all that is not centered on God gives a person the freedom to focus exclusively on God. Teresa does not seek detachment from all created things because she thinks they are evil. No! Rather, detachment is a form of integration in which nothing is an end in itself but everything is united in single-hearted dedication to God. Detachment from everything as ends in themselves is desirable since the world's values are all trivia. Detachment begins with one's own comfort, satisfactions, and health, and it avoids constant complaining. One should also desire to be detached from one's own will, desires, and appetites. This will include giving up rank, status, social acceptance, and the esteem of others. It should also include the abandoning of the never ending search for security in its many forms.

Humility (*Way of Perfection* chps. 15-18). Humility is closely linked to detachment for we must see ourselves as we are and become detached from false selves. This includes avoiding constantly making excuses for oneself. However, humility is particularly necessary in preparing oneself for God's gift of contemplation, and also necessary when God grants contemplation to others but not to oneself. One must always humbly live the path in life that God gives. This includes humbly accepting God's favors and humbly accepting when we are without them. Humility lived with fortitude brings us to the truth about ourselves.

Reflections on the nature and stages of prayer (*Way of Perfection* chps 19-25). When Teresa writes the *Way* in 1566 she is in the stage of the sixth mansion (1562-72), the prayer of union and ecstasy. She sees this prayer as water that refreshes, cleanses, and satisfies, as it draws a person to perfect contemplation. Teresa is keen to speak about the call to contemplation and sees it as a universal invitation and call from God. While many of us would probably start with vocal prayer and move to meditation and then on to contemplation, Teresa starts with the prayer of union in perfect contemplation, then speaks of meditation, and finally of vocal prayer. She sees all prayer from the perspective of contemplation. Teresa is convinced that God invites everyone to follow the path to reach the fountain and union in perfect contemplation. Each one must proceed with determination and never stop pursuing this goal. A person should encourage anyone he or she knows to take up this journey without fear. It will take courage to start, but beginning well is the most important part a person can contribute to this journey. Every step will require "a determined determination." A person should never give up and when necessary find and accept help from others. One should not just follow the crowd, rather follow one's own conscience, and in humility and detachment face up to any obstacles that come one's way.

Teresa goes on to deal with the nature of mental prayer. In mental prayer we think about who we are and to whom we are speaking, so that we appreciate what and how we need to communicate. This is equally true in vocal prayer—individual or communal—or meditation. In prayer we are speaking with God, all powerful and yet lover and friend. It is a communion between friends, and becoming aware of this is itself an awesome experience. It is important, as we have seen, to begin with determination, but determination must characterize every step on the journey. This determination shows our response and appreciation of God's loving generosity to us, it helps us oppose evil, and it enables us to find the courage we need to persevere.

Since some people get nervous at the thought of mental prayer or contemplation, Teresa speaks of the value of vocal prayer when linked to love and recited in inner solitude. Clearly, vocal prayer cannot be reduced to merely reciting words, but one must pray with awareness of the one in whose presence we find ourselves and to whom we are speaking. So, for Teresa, there is a natural link or development from vocal prayer to mental prayer. She goes even further to speak of the connection between vocal prayer and contemplation. When one speaks to God in vocal prayer with attention, love, and inner solitude, God may well raise up such a one to contemplation, suspending a person's faculties—intellect, memory, and will. Gradually, instead of each of us doing the work, God takes over and becomes the one working in us, giving us new understanding and love without us knowing how. God has been listening to us all the time and now replies in extraordinary ways.

Commentary on the "Our Father"

Use a simple method in prayer. In this section it seems that Teresa is speaking to each of us personally. She tells us when you pray the "Our Father," each of you should represent the Lord beside you as teacher and friend, close by you in love, humbly and faithfully guiding you. Remember to ask the Lord for this friendship, and then do not think much but love much, never taking your eyes off the Lord who loves you and wants all that is good for you. When you rejoice see the Lord rejoicing with you; when you are sad see him in his sadness too. It seems he wants and needs our love, so always journey in his company. Recollect all your senses and look at the Lord and communicate with him frequently, not imagining him, but rather being present to him. Use whatever aids are available, an image, a book, anything that can help you draw near to the Lord. Thus, this prayer of recollection leads to intimate friendship—it is not a technique but a growing relationship. You should recollect yourself and attentively respond to the Lord, listening, sharing, and loving. You must do this often so that you form a habit.

> "[T]he recitation of this prayer ('Our Father') must be informed by Teresa's method, which she calls the prayer of recollection. She calls it 'recollection' because 'the soul collects its faculties together and enters within itself to be with its God' (W. 28.4). What is necessary along with this centering of attention is the realization that God is very close. She insists on the nearness of God to each one. . . . Her method is one of presence, of being fully present to God in our prayer, for he is fully present to us at all times."[8]

Our Father (*Way of Perfection*, chps. 26-27: Preparations for prayer). When you think of God as a Father, a first reaction must be to marvel at such an awesome revelation in Christianity. Jesus teaches us this—God acts like a father to each of us, and we become sons and daughters with the only Son. What an extraordinary gesture of love. But you must daily recognize God as Father and live accordingly. This awareness can overwhelm you but it can also lead you to deepen your prayer.

Who art in heaven (*Way of Perfection*, chps. 28-29: The prayer of recollection). Thinking about heaven helps to slow down and recollect the soul. Heaven is wherever the Father is, and that means also deep within your heart, for God is always near enough to hear you. You must enter within yourself and there find God and commune as with your Father. In recollection a person collects all his or her faculties together and enters within himself or herself in solitude to be with God. This will lead to the prayer of quiet as a recollected person withdraws senses and faculties from interest in anything else except God. At first this recollection takes effort, especially in opposing distractions, but with time it becomes effortless. Finding God within your heart means you must prepare yourself for such a guest by emptying your heart of everything else. Thus, you give yourself completely to God and gain a new awareness of your relationship to God and who you are capable of becoming.

For a recollected person appreciation by others is of no importance. However, within one's deepest center one enjoys a companionship with God. This recollection is something one desires and achieves alone with God's help of course—in other words it is acquired. It is a contribution you can personally make, withdrawing from interest in everything else to be with God within your inner spirit. This will include struggles as you try to center all senses and faculties on God, but you will also experience the satisfaction of encounter.

Hallowed be thy name, thy kingdom come (*Way of Perfection*, chps. 30-31: The prayer of quiet). These two phrases of the "Our Father" go together. A person must understand what he or she is asking for in prayer. In the Kingdom one no longer takes earthly things into consideration, but focuses and rejoices in peaceful, love-filled awareness that God is sanctified. Although this is for the next life there are times when God calms our faculties and quiets our spirit so as to anticipate life in the Kingdom. Teresa is talking about vocal prayer lived with recollection which she insists can lead to contemplation—what she describes as initial contemplation, the prayer of quiet.

The prayer of quiet is supernatural, a prayer one cannot earn by one's own efforts. God calms all the faculties and places a person in peace in God's presence. In this experience you will understand in a new way—without the use of the senses—that you are close to God and close to union in divine life in the Kingdom—although not fully there yet. The will is now centered exclusively on God and the other faculties are more focused than ever but not as totally as the will. So, one can continue with daily duties but can feel in a fog!

This prayer of quiet comes and goes as the Lord determines, and there is nothing one can do about it. A person receives it with gratitude and nurtures it in solitude. The intellect will continue to distract and torment the will's exclusive focus on God. However, one finds great peace in this experience, even though one may not understand what is happening. One does feel already invited to the Kingdom. At this time, you must want to remain in this peaceful presence with the Lord, and then the Lord will draw you into deeper union.

Thy will be done on earth as it is in heaven (*Way of Perfection*, chp. 32: The prayer of union). What does the Son want from us that he can give to the Father? Each of us must abandon his or her own will and live in conformity with the will of God—a hard choice if we take it seriously. When the Lord sees a person has strength, commitment, and willingness to suffer, he works his will in such a one. If you approach this dedication with determination and complete willingness, the Lord will call you to share in his cross and passion in order to show the depth of your love.

When a person gives himself or herself completely and surrenders his or her will to God, the Lord allows the person to drink from the fountain of life which is perfect contemplation. In this prayer of union of wills one does nothing and God does everything. God becomes one with that person and transforms him or her into divine union, bringing delights and revealing divine secrets. As a person gives himself or herself totally to God—in thoughts, desire, and hopes, God gives self totally to that person.

Give us this day our daily bread (*Way of Perfection*, chps. 33-35: Eucharist). Constantly doing the Father's will is difficult, and one needs help to do this faithfully with love and courage. Jesus helps each person by remaining with him or her every day in the Eucharist, where he is both example and support in doing the Father's will. Jesus remains present every day, supporting in every trial and suffering, and bringing each person to the joy and consolation of union. A person is never without him and so never needs to be concerned about daily needs, for the Lord will take care of the one he loves. The Lord nourishes us, not with material bread but with a new knowledge that satisfies and sustains each of us on the journey. In fact, in Eucharistic communion Jesus is with you now in that very moment, recognize him in faith and enjoy his companionship. The prayer of recollection after Communion is a very helpful way of being close to the Lord, of sharing in his sufferings, and valuing his love.

Forgive us our trespasses (*Way of Perfection*, chps. 36-37: Forgiveness). One who wants the Father's will to be achieved in him or her should also live with real forgiveness to others. One seeks the Lord's forgiveness—an extraordinary request, and in return offers forgiveness to others—a minor gesture. Often one can feel offended over minor wrongs done and think forgiveness refers to these trivial affronts, lack of respect or esteem. However, when offended in ways that matter a person should forgive with love, happy to share in suffering with the Lord. Contemplatives are humble, forgetful of self, and unaffected by injuries, small or great. In the prayer of union a person finds a resolute desire to forgive. Having been tested in trials and suffering gives a contemplative a realistic approach to his or her own sinfulness and what might offend others does not offend a contemplative person, but simply offers a way of accompanying the suffering, offended Lord. One who knows how much he or she has been forgiven can easily forgive others.

Certainly, the "Our Father" is a wonderful evangelical prayer that responds to each one's needs. It brings so many blessings and favors to each person. It demands two things from a person who seeks the Lord—he or she should give over his or her will to God and practice forgiveness. The more perfectly one accepts these two responsibilities the more one advances in prayer. You must recite this prayer with sincerity and resolve.

And lead us not into temptation but deliver us from evil (*Way of Perfection*, chps. 38-41: Temptations). One who gives himself or herself to a life of prayer does not ask to be freed from trials, struggles, or temptations. Rather, such a one is happy to face these trials as a sign of love for God. One fights against temptations with the strength the Lord gives. But there are some enemies of spiritual progress that it is appropriate to fear. In growth and consolation one must be aware of a breakdown in humility. Some can even think they have virtue when they do not, others grow careless because of the consolations they feel or the virtues they think they have. Another challenge is the lack of consistency in practicing virtue. If you live in humility the Lord will always be there to help you.

A serious temptation prayerful people need to confront is when they live with a false sense of humility, feeling unworthy about one thing or another, or stressing too much their own sins and failures. True humility brings peace not disturbance and teaches one to focus on God's mercy. Part of false humility is an exaggerated sense of one's ascetical commitment and false sense of confidence that one will not fall back into former failings. You should entrust yourself to the Father's love and ask to be guarded against these treacheries.

To resist the serious temptations that a contemplative person can face he or she needs to live in love and with fear of the Lord—the former quickens one's step and the latter makes one watch carefully his or her every step. These are the two remedies for all temptations. A contemplative loves truth and whatever is worthy of love. Teresa said that those who love see the world differently than those who do not—they look at everything through the lens of love. Love is the key quality that manifests the intensity of one's prayer. It likewise is the quality that helps one discern the deceptions and illusions of a loveless life.

Fear of the Lord is easily recognized in a dedicated person. At first it might be barely discernible, but with progress in the spiritual life and prayer it becomes an evident aspect of one's life. It protects one from sinful situations. Fear of the Lord linked to fortitude leads a person to a very deliberate approach to life that helps one become careful and attentive in daily life, sensitive to the gravity of sin, and careful regarding occasions and situations that lead to sin. This reverence is easy for those who love, and love protects itself with fear of the Lord. Contemplatives whose lives evidence these two virtues have a positive effect on others, maintain conversations focused on goodness, decrease judgment of others, and encourage people they meet through their agreeable social interactions. Love and a sense of wonder and awe help one advance on the spiritual journey with calmness and security.

But deliver us from evil (*Way of Perfection*, chp. 42: Longing to be free from evil and to be with God). Jesus longed to be free from the burdens of living in a world of unbelief, cruelty, and sinfulness. Likewise the Lord wants each of us to be free from evil forever. One always wants to be free of all present evil but in this life it is not possible, and we all remain weary of this life's burdens. Contemplatives in their prayer receive so much from the Lord they long to be with him forever. To be peacefully satisfied in this world would require everything to change—our values, desires, and hopes are often opposite to God's.

The "Our Father" contains so many deep secrets and prepares us for union with God. We must follow the path of spiritual life contained in the teachings of this prayer and it will lead us to the fountain of living water. There we encounter Our Lord in whom we discover every good we speak of, think about, and do. Amen.

A few final thoughts from Teresa

- Your life must be focused on love, an integrated commitment of every aspect of life, lived in the reality of your own humility.
- When in prayer God gives you a clear knowledge, you will have a different view of reality, and you will love God and others in a different way.
- You are not journeying forward in prayer, rather God is drawing you to divine life.
- God grants you deeper prayer and never ceases to bestow loving gifts until you reach higher degrees of union.
- The Lord invites all; your task is to persevere in your commitment.
- You must have a great and very resolute determination to persevere in prayer.
- Your prayer must be deep recollection that will prepare you to think, to speak, to listen, and to receive.
- Any harm in your life of prayer will come from not truly understanding that you live in the presence of love; God is always near you.

Chapter Six

The Interior Castle

This is a very important book in the history of spirituality. St. Teresa of Avila wrote this extraordinary book in 1577. She entered the last stage of the mystical life in 1572 and died in 1582. The *Interior Castle* is the most mature work that Teresa wrote. Moreover, this is the most systematic and ordered presentation of the spiritual theology of Saint Teresa. The *Autobiography* was very much focused on Teresa's spiritual experiences, and the *Way of Perfection* was a teaching aid for her sisters. But in the *Interior Castle* Teresa integrates perfectly both experience and doctrinal principals. While the *Autobiography* focuses on what happened to Teresa in the contemplative and mystical periods of her spiritual life, and the *Way of Perfection* is her principal ascetical work, the *Interior Castle* presents a balanced coordination of ascetical life and mystical life. From a pedagogical and literary point of view this is Teresa's masterpiece. This book is complementary to the other two; it takes up stages one to three of the *Way of Perfection* and deals with stages four to six of the *Autobiography*. The *Interior Castle* is primarily a pedagogical work, and it is very useful to those who have not yet reached the later stages in the mystical life.

The origin and development of the *Interior Castle*

The year 1577 was a difficult one for Teresa. She was very unwell, as she tells us in the prologue to the *Interior Castle*. She had suffered from headaches and other sicknesses for over three months. Also, it was a year of terrible pressures from conflicting authorities, some even trying to undo all the work of the Reform. In 1576, Fr. Jerónimo Tostado arrived in Spain as a special Visitator, sent to oversee the faithful implementation of the decrees of the Carmelite General Chapter in Piacenza. He was clearly against the Reform, and only the interventions of the papal nuncio, who suggested that Tostado begin his work in Portugal, protected the convents of the Reform. However, the Papal nuncio, Nicolás Ormaneto, a great supporter of Teresa, died in June 1577, and was replaced with opponents of the Reform, including Jerónimo Tostado and his successor, Felipe Sega. Exhausted, Teresa entered a kind of self-imprisonment in the convent of St. Joseph's. Even the temporary peace she experienced there was interrupted when she was elected prioress of the convent of the Incarnation in 1577. However, her enemies opposed that too, so at least she was left alone for a while in St. Joseph's. In the midst of all these pressures, physical and psychological, Teresa wrote her masterpiece, the *Interior Castle*. The idea to write this book started with a discussion in Toledo between Teresa and her frequent confessor and provincial, Fr. Gracían. The number of convents had increased to twelve and the need for formation became urgent. Unfortunately, the *Autobiography* was still in the hands of the Inquisition and unavailable to the nuns. Fr. Gracían decided Teresa should write a new book on prayer. Since Teresa was not supportive of this idea, Fr. Gracían made Teresa's confessor at the time, Dr. Velázquez, impose this project on Teresa. The immediate reason for this was fear that the *Autobiography* and its important teachings would be lost in the Inquisition. So, basically, Gracían was trying to save those teachings in the *Autobiography* that he considered to be of universal value. Teresa started her work on the feast of the Holy Trinity, June 2nd, 1577 and within a month—in spite of constant interruptions and pressures—she had already completed the first four mansions. In July, Teresa left Toledo to return to Avila, where she left the book aside for almost five months. In November she picked it up again and by November 29th, the eve of the feast of St. Andrew, 1577, she had finished the *Interior Castle*, writing more than half of it at St. Joseph's in less than a month! We have Teresa's hand-written copy of this masterpiece which is the first draft and the final text. Although Teresa expressed aversion to beginning this work she ended up happy she had done it and pleased with her work (C. Epilogue 1).

Commenting on Mother Teresa as the great teacher of prayer, Fr. Steven Payne suggests the following characteristics of her spirituality: 1. A compelling conviction that God is real and active in our lives. 2. A strong ecclesial dimension. 3. The importance of human friendship as a support on the spiritual journey. 4. An intense devotion to the humanity of Christ."[9]

This book is not the result of any direct or specific spiritual, mystical experience of Teresa that she wished to share with her sisters. In fact, in the prologue she states that she has no desire to write the book, overwhelmed as she felt with sickness, conflicts, and misunderstanding. Teresa entered the last stage of the mystical life around 1572 and mystical experiences continued throughout the writing of this book. She suggested to the nuns that they could think about the soul as a castle made entirely out of diamond (C. 1.1, 2). Also, one of her biographers, Diego de Yepes, testified that Teresa while staying at an inn in Arévalo on her way from Medina del Campo to Avila, told him that she had a vision of a castle. These references do not seem to be the basis for the book. Moreover, in writing the *Interior Castle*, she had no direct dependence on any other book she had previously read. This book is the matured integration of a series of mystical experiences over many years and the important doctrinal positions involved. This is an original and personal work. It is written for her nuns and also for some theologians interested in the spiritual and mystical life. It is principally a mystical-contemplative work and deals with the later stages in the mystical life.

Some basic ideas and principal themes in the *Interior Castle*

When Teresa wrote the *Interior Castle* she had advanced beyond her experiences and understanding contained in the *Autobiography,* and she had clarified her interpretation of the various stages. When she wrote the *Autobiography* in 1565 she was in the fifth mansion and as she wrote it began to enter the sixth. She wrote the *Way of Perfection* a year later in 1566. Some of the basic ideas or experiences that Teresa wrote about in her previous works she expands and clarifies in the *Interior Castle*. She speaks about the presence of God, God's life in the soul, and the mutual presence of a person and God to one another. She addresses again the value of prayer and especially the value of a life of prayer as a way to God. She insists yet again on the importance of clear convictions regarding interior values and the transformative influence of grace in the mystical life. She further teaches that all spiritual life is a life of two, a relationship of friendship based on interiorization and recollection. For Teresa, holiness is always union with God, and includes contemplation of the presence of God in everything and in oneself. This leads her to repeat her vision of the indwelling of the Trinity in the lives of the just.

> *When we read Teresa's Interior Castle we discover that the time we spend in prayer is not as important as what happens to us in that time.*

This is a book on prayer. Its focus is not on the ascetical life but on the mystical life. It shows less interest in the process and stresses the end of the journey. In developing her thought, Teresa presents two principal arguments which also become the structure of the work. First, she deals with the evolution of the spiritual life from the liberation from sin to the state of consummated union—this takes places in seven stages. Second, she deals with the stages of prayer growth as a form of life that enriches our ability to relate to God—these stages become the seven mansions. Moreover, in dealing with these two principal themes Teresa touches on many connected topics, such as virtues, grace, and the apostolic value of interior life.

The structure of the *Interior Castle*

This book presents the unity of the spiritual life in a dynamic vision. This literary, doctrinal, and pedagogical masterpiece is structured on allegories. It is made up of seven stages and can be divided into two parts.

Stages 1-3 describe the natural life, in other words it is the ascetical part.

Stages 4-7 describe the supernatural life, in other words it is the mystical part.

It is also possible to view the book in a threefold division.

Stages 1-3 are the ascetical part and focuses on sin—purification and liberation .

Stages 3-5 are a transition section

Stages 5-7 are the mystical part and focuses on anti-sin—the reception of the gift of holiness.

The whole book develops with a background of allegory, and the allegories help to structure the book and provide a general plan. Some of Teresa's favorite allegories that she mentions in other books appear in this book too. She speaks of a castle, both as a protection of the military castle and as a wonderful and beautiful castle of crystal. Of course, she also uses the seven rings of a castle's walls to portray the seven dwelling places. She uses the allegory of battle that can lead to victory and can bring peace. She speaks of darkness and light. Then as elsewhere Teresa uses the allegories of fountains of water, one at a distance implying the work of transporting the water, and the other as a fountain that gushes forth from the ground. She uses the former to refer to meditative, discursive prayer, and the latter to contemplation. Teresa also introduces the allegory of the deaf mute, and presents it in three stages. At first a person is both deaf and dumb, unable to hear the voice of the Lord or to speak to him. Second, a person is no longer deaf but still dumb. Third the person is neither deaf nor dumb. An allegory that Teresa really likes is that of the silk worm and she uses it in two ways. First she uses it to describe two stages in prayer, the worm that crawls becomes an image of meditation, and the butterfly that breaks out of the cocoon to go forth in flight refers to contemplation. However, she also uses this same image for all seven stages in the spiritual life and the life of prayer. So, she describes the birth of the worm, how it begins to eat, and how it grows. Then the worm enters a cocoon and sleeps in quiet, it dies, breaks out as a butterfly, and dies again consumed by the light and heat of the flame. A final allegory to mention is that of matrimony and its three stages of dating or courtship, engagement, and matrimony.

The Interior Castle

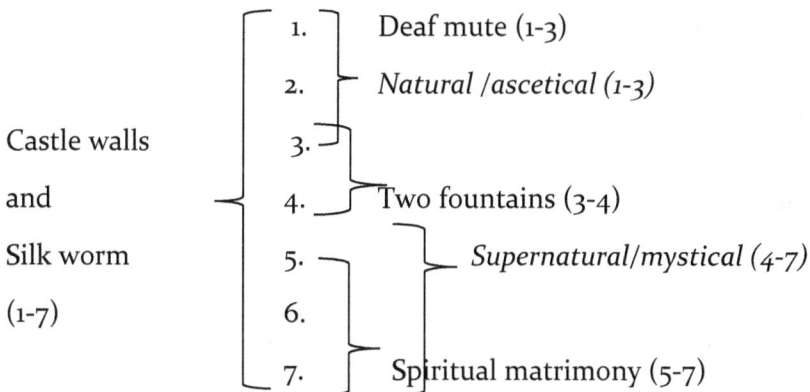

	1.	Deaf mute (1-3)
	2.	*Natural /ascetical (1-3)*
Castle walls	3.	
and	4.	Two fountains (3-4)
Silk worm	5.	*Supernatural/mystical (4-7)*
(1-7)	6.	
	7.	Spiritual matrimony (5-7)

These allegories help Teresa describe the seven stages in the spiritual life and the accompanying seven stages in the life of prayer.

Spiritual life-

1. From sin through difficulties and fight to the life of grace
2. First developments in the spiritual life, along with awareness of dangers
3. One begins to obey the demands of grace
4. The fight continues, and the spiritual interventions of God begin
5. Union with God begins, first spiritual graces regarding the humanity of Christ
6. Still semi-passive, the interior reform by God, purification and visions
7. Full union with the Trinity leading to apostolic fruitfulness

Life of prayer-

1. Simple forms of prayer
2. Discursive and meditative prayer
3. Normal and perfect meditation
4. Beginnings of mystical contemplation
5. Perfect mystical contemplation (and phenomena)
6. Ecstatic prayer
7. Perfect mystical contemplation and the stable presence of God

Teresa's teachings on prayer in the *Interior Castle* (a summary)

First mansion: Simple vocal prayer plus reflection

When we begin the spiritual journey, it is important that we know ourselves well and appreciate our calling to be a dwelling place for God and recipients of God's extraordinary graces. As a dwelling place for God each of us should go deeper within ourselves in prayer and reflection. This prayer and reflection can accompany our vocal prayer, helping us realize who we are and to whom we are speaking—namely God. Of course, serious sin blocks our ability to enter these dwelling places and makes everything we do sin-filled and unworthy of God's invitation to dwell together. However, irrespective of our sins God always dwells within us but we can block God's grace within us by our sinful lives. We all need a healthy fear and profound humility to be able to enter into the inner dwelling places. However, the more important part in our spiritual journey is not what we are doing but what God is doing in us. Self-knowledge prepares us for all that lies ahead, and as we journey inward we must constantly practice mutual love. Unfortunately, in this first dwelling place we must face so many temptations, distractions, and threats to humility that we do not see much of the light that comes from the Lord who is in the central dwelling place deep within us. Our part is to balance self-knowledge with a humble awareness of God's call to enter all the dwelling places to which the Lord calls us.

Second mansion: Occasional meditation.

If we respond to the call and challenge in the first mansion, we can move on to the second. But this needs determination and often we remain attached to, and do not avoid, the occasions of sin. With God's mercy we can strive to recognize and then escape these temptations. This stage is more difficult than the first, for we now hear the Lord calling us and feel the attraction of his love. The Lord's call can come through others, through reading good books, through sermons, and in experiences of trials, illness, and of course prayer. We must remind ourselves of the importance of perseverance throughout this stage in our spiritual lives. It is a time when we can confront temptations and the false values of a lost world, first through the aid, and then through the initial purification, of the faculties of intellect, memory, and will. Although this is only the second mansion, we need God's help, compassionate care, and enlightenment to move on. It is also true that we can be strengthened in our resolve by keeping company with those whose interests and hopes are like our own. We need determination in faith, give no importance to spiritual consolation, and seek the will of God in everything we do. Moreover, we should not become discouraged in failure, but continue our efforts in peace, trusting always in the compassion of the Lord. We can consult learned guides when necessary, but above all we must persevere in prayer, deepen self-knowledge, and never turn back in our spiritual journey.

Third mansion: Habitual meditation

We are blessed if and when we enter the third dwelling place and leave behind all the temptations and insecurity of the second mansion. Having reached this third stage we should avoid offending the Lord in any way, great or small, practice self-control, and give ourselves to recollection and prayer. It is not enough to have good desires, nor should we think that our good desires should earn us spiritual growth and satisfaction. Rather, we must humbly accept and let God's will prevail in us at all times. For our part we should stress perseverance and detachment from everything that does not lead us to God. When we reach this stage we must be careful not to cling to it, disillusioned by a little progress, and become shocked by further trials the Lord feels are necessary for us. We must avoid self-deception regarding our presumed progress and give ourselves always to the pursuit of God's will. We should strive to practice virtue, surrender ourselves to God's will, and maintain humility, patience, and perseverance. This spiritual journey is wearisome, filled with threats of false humility and immature desires for consolations. If we focus on ourselves we can drag out this stage more than it needs. However, if we abandon ourselves to God's will in gratitude and in prompt obedience, God will give us the humility, fortitude, and love needed in this third dwelling place.

Fourth mansion: Prayer of quiet

Mansions one to three describe the ascetical stages in spiritual life. Mansion four begins the supernatural and mystical stages of life. The experiences of mansion four are ineffable and indescribable, and generally we only enter this dwelling place after spending a long time travelling through the first three. We will still have to deal with temptations, but they are rarely harmful, and in fact they can strengthen us and increase our humility as they help us maintain a healthy perspective on our life and growth. Even in mansions one to three some everyday experiences bring us joy and consolation; these are experiences we acquire. They come in happy events of daily life, but can also come in our prayer. They start with us and our satisfactions, even though they may end in God as we express gratitude for these natural reactions. However, mansion four incudes many delightful experiences that begin with God and then end by the body sharing in these delights. Consolations that begin in human experience do not expand our hearts; rather we can become attached to them and sad when they are not there. These consolations are typical in the previous dwelling places and seem to result from our dedicated efforts in meditation. However, authentic love does not result from consolations but from pursuing God's will in everything. This love can be strengthened with the aid of the faculties of intellect, memory, and will, even though we are distracted by the wanderings of the imagination—something that causes us lots of pain. Our main responsibility at this time is not to think much but to love much.

Quite different from the consolations, both natural and spiritual, that we experience in life in the first three mansions are the delights we experience from God in the prayer of quiet. The former come in meditation, the latter in contemplation— gifts of God that we experience passively in the deepest center of our being, even though they end by reaching the body too, which then shares in the delights of the soul. These delights received in prayer overwhelm all our faculties in union with

God. We cannot acquire these gifts but can prepare for them in humility and detachment. In fact, we should not even strive for these gifts but accept God's sovereign will in these matters. This prayer of quiet brings a sense of freedom from fear, a desire for further purification, a deeper sense of one's own sinfulness, a rejection of the evil aspects of the world, and a growth in virtue. Our task at this time is to avoid all occasions of sin. Our lack of understanding of what is happening to us at this stage can lead to a lot of pain. Distractions can be everywhere but they do not need to hinder prayer.

Before we experience the prayer of quiet there comes the prayer of recollection. (Here, Teresa considers the prayer of recollection as infused, passive, and supernatural, whereas in the *Way of Perfection* she dealt with a recollection that was acquired). Our senses and faculties, having focused on other interests for a long time, now seem to be losing their interest in all external things. God recognizes our good will and gently draws us to life in this fourth dwelling place. We must seek God within our hearts and not in creatures, listening and being attentive to God's loving invitation. Distractions will remain and should not upset us, for all this is God's work—awakening love within us. This prayer is not acquired by us thinking about God or by using our imagination to focus on God. This prayer does not come when we want it but when God wants it for us. We should think less, try to control the wanderings of the intellect, and never try to force this prayer but live with total disinterest and resignation to God's will. It is better not to strive to understand this recollection but to leave it in God's hands. Our contribution could include thinking less, acting less, decreasing our efforts, focusing on God's honor and glory, becoming forgetful of ourselves, and concentrating on God's presence within us. This prayer of recollection generally precedes the prayer of quiet and becomes an entrance into the fourth mansion.

> *Throughout her teachings Teresa insists on the importance of focusing on the humanity of Christ. "Pivots of Teresian christology are the humanity and divinity of Jesus, the Cross and Resurrection, not excluding the other mysteries of his earthly life, and then a remarkable set of 'presences' of the Risen Lord—in his Church, in the Eucharist, in the community, and in one's innermost self."[10]*

Fifth mansion: Prayer of simple union

This fifth mansion is a wonderful experience and it is almost impossible to describe it. The Lord intends this gift for many but few prepare themselves for it. Great commitment is needed in the practice of virtue, along with great care even in small things. A person must give every aspect of his or her life to God, all faculties be passive to everything except God, and one totally surrendered to God's will. Unlike the previous mansion, one's experience of union in the fifth completely includes the suspension of all three faculties of intellect, memory, and will. When this union happens a person knows with certainty that it is from God. Although this union is complete, it can have various degrees of intensity. Our contribution to this stage is insignificant, but God's transforming action is wonderful to appreciate. A silkworm spins and then dies in a cocoon, and a beautiful butterfly emerges. So too, our little efforts to rid ourselves of self-love, self-will, and attachments, together with our penance, prayer, obedience, and virtues—all help us die in the cocoon. In this prayer of union, a butterfly emerges and we cannot even recognize ourselves. This union produces a spirit of penance, solitude, attachment, zeal for God's glory, and a longing to please God. A person in this dwelling place finds no peace or interest in anything but God, and lives in painful longing to be always in this union. One also suffers intensely from awareness of sin in the world and the horror of God being so profoundly offended. In this union God imprints new life on the soul, like a seal pressed into wax, and one receives this gift of divine life.

When someone does not receive the supernatural gifts of this stage, he or she should not feel without hope. Rather, a person in this mansion must proceed in the service of the Lord, in increased self-knowledge, and in fidelity to the will of God. This itself is a union of wills and even though it does not include the supernatural delights it can be a step towards it. Nothing in the world disturbs this person as he or she works through suffering towards a death that brings transformation. In the prayer of union God effects this death and transformation, whereas in earlier mansions we seek to effect it by our striving for God's will in our ascetical choices. Searching for God's will, we must work for love of God and love of neighbor. It is love of neighbor that shows how much we love God, but our love of neighbor is rooted in our love for God. Our part is empathy, compassion, delight in others' success, and doing whatever we can to show love to our neighbor. Like the butterfly, one never stops to find a resting place. This prayer of union is like a courtship in which future spouses get to know each other, find happiness in each other's company, and realize that fulfillment lies in being together. At this time one must be especially careful not to place oneself in occasions of sin, but pray for God's constant, strong support. We should be watchful over our practice of virtue and our dedication to love of neighbor, for growth can never be at a standstill and love is never idle.

Sixth mansion: Mystical engagement

Having had a taste of union in the courtship of the fifth mansion, one longs for this union again and hopes that it becomes permanent. There arises in the lover a painful longing, intensified by the Lord's plan not to fulfill a person's desires too soon, but to let one appreciate how important this encounter is by letting one suffer intensely the pain and sickness of unfulfilled love. The pain and suffering of this stage take on many forms. It might be the ridicule and gossip of others who are jealous of a person's spiritual growth, but for a dedicated person praise or criticism are the same, for he or she gives all glory to God for the gifts received. Sometimes a person at this stage has to deal with physical pain and sickness, and while this is less than the psychological and spiritual pains and trials, it is still a trial and taste of martyrdom. A further trial comes from an inexperienced confessor who thinks every unusual spiritual experience results from some form of depression and should be rejected. This painful situation intensifies when one is not able to explain one's experiences clearly and must live in misunderstanding and doubt. Only the Lord can free one from this oppression, but in the meantime a person learns how helpless he or she is without God's help. At this time, the problem is that one begins to question one's love for God, to see one's own misery, and to feel one can no longer pray. All this contributes to God's purification of a person who longs for union in love.

In spite of these trials, the Lord also makes a person realize how completely he or she belongs to God. Very gentle impulses or wounds of love touch the substance or deepest center of a person's being, awakening a person's love. One knows something special has happened even without understanding it. This painful but satisfying experience is like a spark of divine love that touches one's heart but is not strong enough to set it on fire—that is for later—and so one is still left in intensely painful longing. No one can achieve this experience; it is pure gift from God who seeks to enrich a person with the divine presence and love.

At this time one can also experience locutions of various kinds, some of which can be false and can easily deceive. Those which are authentic support one's spiritual life, bring peace, find a permanent place in the memory, are brought to fulfillment by the Lord, and bring the Lord's delight to the recipient. To protect oneself from misunderstanding and deception it is always better to seek guidance from a prudent and learned person. Sometimes one can hear the Lord's message in an intellectual vision. In these latter cases the locution is so clear one remembers every word, it is unexpected and distinctly heard, the words are often different than those one normally uses. It is accompanied by profound understanding, one is humbled by this communication, and finally one feels constrained to listen. All these are signs the locution is authentic and comes from God.

A person attains spiritual betrothal in ecstatic experiences that take one out of one's senses. As the Lord sees a person suffer with intense desire, he gives him or her courage and then with an interior communication joins the person to himself. In this experience a person understands something of what is happening and becomes fully awake to the things of

God, and in this suspension feels carried away and then receives special communications and revelations. Although a person does not remember these extraordinary communications they have a definite transformative impact in the depths of one's spirit. When this experience of ecstasy passes, one's will remains absorbed in love, and one's intellect withdrawn from anything that does not lead to love. One longs only to love God in every way possible. The whole person is now betrothed to God within the center of his or her being.

A further kind of ecstasy occurs when God with a powerful impulse of love carries off a soul that has given himself or herself completely to God. A huge wave overwhelms the person who has no ability to react in any way. Great courage is necessary, for this experience can be frightening as one sees one's own spirit go forth from the body. In this ecstasy God communicates in a new way, offering visions of life beyond this one. When one emerges from this ecstasy one feels gifted by God, senses little attraction to anything except God, deepens self-knowledge in humility, and finds nothing but pain in living in this world. Wearied of everything except God, a person now lives with longing for God alone. Enriched by further ecstasies, the soul abandons itself to God, accepts whatever pain life brings, and feels filled with zeal to serve God and others—to do anything that gives praise to God.

With the increase in the blessings of God comes a deeper awareness of one's sins and profound sorrow for them, especially with an awareness of one's ingratitude and unworthiness. As a person understands more the greatness of God, so too he or she sees personal sinfulness and becomes afraid of offending God or losing God. Even though drawn to higher levels of union in mansion six, one should never stop reflecting on the humanity of Christ, for Jesus is our guide through these various dwelling places. The delights of this stage give place to time and opportunity when one can return to reflecting on the humanity of Christ, as long as one does not get too focused on discursive prayer. Often the will is not completely dead and can be rekindled in love by this practice. At this time the Lord Jesus communicates through visions; these are not imaginative visions that use the senses but intellectual visions in which a person feels Jesus is present but does not see him. They can last a short time or many months, when a person senses Jesus is always at his or her side. Moreover, a person in this continual companionship is immersed in peace and absolute conviction that this vision is authentic.

At times the Lord communicates through an imaginative vision in which one sees the humanity of the Lord. This vision is intense but short lived and while an image it is real and frightening to the recipient. This is not the result of one's imagination when one creates the image, rather this imaginative vision is complete gift, unexpected—a communication of life that leaves one enriched and at peace. God grants these visions, as and when God desires. At times the Lord places a person in a moment's suspension and in that brief ecstasy reveals secrets of the divine life, truths about God and our relationship to divine life.

The many favors of the Lord enrich a person but also leave him or her in greater pain and longing to be permanently with the Lord. At this time the lover feels a painful blow or wound as if suddenly hit or pierced by an arrow in his or her very substance—the most interior part of one's spirit. All the faculties of intellect, memory, and will are held in suspension as they willingly suffer this pain of absence, gratitude, longing, and unfulfilled love. One's entire being is wracked with pain, not in the body but in the spirit, yet it is a pain one treasures. The pain can last a few hours but is so intense one can long for death. Nevertheless, this experience produces great benefit to the person.

Seventh mansion: Mystical matrimony

After the sixth mansion the Lord grants spiritual matrimony to his spouse and brings her into the seventh mansion and unites himself to her more deeply than at any other time. In this union, a person sees the Holy Spirit in intellectual vision, and what was previously understood in faith is now communicated and now seen, for the Trinity dwells within such a person. In this experience a person is not outside himself or herself but more occupied in the service of God than ever, and still remains in union with the Trinity. This has a transforming, beneficial effect on a person. The spiritual matrimony takes place in the center of one's inner spirit, and in this experience God communicates great and sublime secrets. God and the lover are united, the two become one, they cannot be separated, and the person understands clearly that God now gives him or her new life. A person now feels secure and yet prudently maintains fear of falling away; he or she is at peace even when surrounded by trials and fatigues. The results of union in the seventh mansion include forgetfulness of self, appreciation of one's own helplessness, a desire to suffer for love, increased dedication to serve the Lord, and a desire for death to enter greater union. At the same time a person in this stage has no interest in consolations, lives in increased detachment, and enjoys the remembrance of the Lord's tender love. This is a time of peace, repose, and security. A person in this seventh mansion is strengthened by the Lord, keeps himself or herself away from all sin, and maintains commitment to the life of virtues. Although no longer experiencing ecstasies, this person is fortified by the blessings of the Lord, and is now totally dedicated to the service of others—all done in love for the Lord.

A few final thoughts from Teresa

- The only door you can use to enter into deeper union with God is prayer.
- It is foolish to think you will enter heaven without having entered into yourself in self-knowledge.
- Perfection in prayer requires love of God and love of neighbor.
- You must realize that you are capable of much more than you can imagine.
- Growth requires of you not to think much but to love much.
- You need to learn to recognize the signs of love all around you.
- Never hold yourself back in your life of prayer; you must make progress.

Chapter Seven

Teresa's *Book of the Foundations*

Introductory notes on *The Book of the Foundations*

The book of the *Foundations* is the least read book of Teresa. It seems to many readers that this book is probably a chronicle, or a simple historical account, or a travel journal. But Teresa is Teresa! And when she communicates it is always in the context of a life of total commitment, spiritual enrichment, deepening prayer, and love. Without this book we would not understand how much Teresa suffered for the extension of the Lord's work. This is the lived experience of her spirituality and describes how the Lord is intimately close to her at all times, guiding her and challenging her in love and service. However, it also gives us a real view of contemplative life as it overflows into daily action, for this book clearly shows Teresa as an outstanding business woman who has to deal with complicated organizations, financial and contractual affairs, contentious and arrogant people, complicated bureaucracies, and competing religious groups. She wades her way through it all while maintaining the life of prayer and contemplation, showing us that prayer is not separate from the struggles and responsibilities of daily life. This book is Teresa's theology and spirituality of ministry.

In February, 1570, while Teresa was in Malagón which was her third foundation, the Lord appeared to her and encouraged her to found as many houses as possible and to write about them (ST 6). The Lord linked this request to the good he said would be done to others. So, from the start Teresa saw this task as achieving two goals; first to give glory to God who was the primary founder of these houses, and secondly to engage in writing about them as a form of ministry of doing good to others. However, she did not begin to write until late in August, 1573, then possibly also due to the encouragement of her confessor at the time, the Jesuit, Fr. Ripalda who had read about the foundation of St. Joseph's in Avila in the *Autobiography*, and thought a history of the other seven monasteries she had founded by 1573 would be of service to the Lord (F. 27.22). In 1573, Teresa was in Salamanca, trying to find a more suitable permanent residence for her nuns who were renting at the time, and while there she started her *Foundations*, completing the first nine chapters. Once Teresa had completed writing about the first seven foundations as requested by Fr. Ripalda, having changed confessors, and being involved in many difficult business matters, she thought of not continuing the writing on the foundations, but Fr. Gracián encouraged her to continue, even if she could only write short sections at a time. Teresa then wrote chapters 20 to 27 and then thought she was definitely finished with the work and wrote a first conclusion at the end of chapter 27, November 11, 1576. However, after 1580 Teresa opened another five houses and writes about them in chapters 28 to 31.

The book of the *Foundations* is essentially an account of the beginnings of the various monasteries, the difficulties Teresa encounters in her travels, in seeking accommodations for the nuns, in dealing with all kinds of authorities and the endless problems some of them present, and at the same time in trying to cope with her increasing illnesses. The opposition she encounters is extraordinary but her tenacity and spirit of sacrifice, linked to her confidence that all these foundations are God's work, makes this a wonderful testimony to Teresa's dedication and the Lord's grace-filled presence to her at all times. Teresa digresses often to give advice to her prioresses, she also gives stories of spiritual courage and dedication of people she met in the course of her work, and never omits to give praise to generous people who collaborated in the foundation work. Needless to say, Teresa always has interest in teaching about prayer, and here too, in Chapters 4-8 she gives a short treatise on prayer and counsels to her prioresses. This treatise is filled with practical advice for those involved in directing others in their spiritual life. She writes about those who are afraid of undertaking the spiritual journey, warns against thinking too much rather than loving much, insists that love of God makes one restless for the good of others, and stresses the importance of obedience to the will of God for growth in the spiritual life. Teresa warns against false mystical experiences, speaks forcefully against the problem of "melancholy," reminds her readers that some mystical revelations and visions are false. Then, she insists that her prioresses practice discretion in leading others in the spiritual life. In fact, throughout Teresa digresses to give advice to her prioresses. Besides her teachings on prayer and her counsels to her prioresses, Teresa frequently inserts stories about the dedication or sacrifice, or perseverance, or generosity of saintly individuals who she presents as models of spiritual commitment. So, the whole book, while faithfully responding to her confessors' directives regarding the historical documentation of the Reform, also presents us with a wonderful and exciting portrayal of spirituality in the real world.

A short history of Teresa's foundations

Teresa writes the *Foundations* following a vision in 1570 and under obedience to her confessor at the time, the Jesuit, Fr. Ripalda. Teresa's accounts are filled with struggles, opposition, and endless problems. I have highlighted some, giving key experiences at the beginning of each foundation. Teresa was also filled with gratitude to people from all walks of life that generously helped her. "[T]he Lord Himself . . . chooses in each place someone to help Him" (F. 29.8). I have given one or two names of the many collaborators who assisted in the foundations. Some were very generous, others not as helpful as they thought or maybe wanted to be. However, the Lord used many to help Teresa in her work and she was always grateful.

St. Joseph's in Medina del Campo (1567). See F. 3.

Facing sacrifices for the first foundation after St. Joseph's in Avila.

Isabel Fontecha, Fr. Antonio de Heredia

St. Joseph's in Avila was founded in 1562 and Teresa reflects how blessed the monastery was with its first nuns' dedication, detachment, spirit of poverty, and obedience. They loved solitude, showed courage, and manifested a great desire to serve and suffer for the Lord. Teresa goes on to speak about her own longing to bring others to the love and service of the Lord and the Lord's consoling words to her.

In February 1567, the General of the Carmelites, Fr. Rubeo, visited Avila. Teresa was at first anxious that he would be displeased with her work of reform and possibly send her back to the monastery of the Incarnation. However, Fr. Rubeo welcomed Teresa, expressed satisfaction with her work, and encouraged her in her ministry, giving permission for other foundations. After his departure, Teresa wrote to Fr. Rubeo, asking permission to open monasteries of the Reform for friars, and Fr. Rubeo granted permission for two.

Teresa proceeded with the founding of a monastery in Medina del Campo. Priests and bishop helped with securing permissions, a young woman, Isabel Fontecha, provided a little money to rent a house, and the prior of the friars in Medina, Fr. Antonio de Heredia, found a place for Teresa and the first six nuns. On the way from Avila the group stopped at Arévalo and discovered that the Augustinian friars who lived near the new foundation opposed it and were ready to start a lawsuit against Teresa and her new foundation. Fr. Báñez, the theologian, and at times confessor to Teresa, felt the problem with the Augustinians could be resolved quickly, and so the group made preparations to enter the house Fr. Heredia had obtained. However, the so-called house turned out to be dilapidated and unsuitable, but with generous gifts from the owner of the property, the nuns moved in. The property turned out to be in worse condition than expected. Local people helped in many ways with offers of temporary housing, funds for re-construction, alms, and food. Soon the nuns had an enclosure and began their community life, and two months later their original house was ready. The nuns lived there for several years. Still interested in opening a monastery of the Reform for friars, Teresa spoke to the prior of Medina, and he asked to become one of the first members of the new foundation. Then along came the future John of the Cross, home in Medina del Campo to celebrate his first Mass, and he, too, offered to join the new community. Meanwhile, the nuns settled, were well respected, and spiritually dedicated, and others came to join them.

St. Joseph's in Malagón (1568). See F. 9.

Appreciating that poverty leads to a rich spiritual life

Doña Luisa de la Cerda

The community in Medina del Campo grew in religious dedication, love, and spirituality, and provided a solid foundation for the future of the Reform. There was a lady in Toledo, Doña Luisa de la Cerda, with whom Teresa had previously spent six months following the death of the lady's husband, who knew Teresa had permission to found other houses and wanted her to found one in her own city of Malagón. Teresa felt the town was too small to support a new community, but others, including Fr. Domingo Báñez, urged Teresa to go ahead. Teresa had wanted her foundations to be without income or endowment, but that was not always possible. In this case Doña Luisa de la Cerda provided support, and after a few days delay, which the nuns spent in her castle, the new community opened on Palm Sunday, 1568.

The Conception of Our Lady of Mount Carmel, Valladolid (1568). See F. 10-12.

Knowing the Lord guides through visions

Don Bernadino de Mendoza and Doña Maria de Mendoza

Five months prior to the foundation in Malagón, Don Bernadino de Mendoza offered Teresa property just outside Valladolid. Teresa, who did not think the property to be suitable, still wanted to make the foundation as soon as possible, moved partly by a vision she had. She arrived in Valladolid on August 10, 1568, and discovered the property would be very expensive to maintain, was too far away from the city and opportunities to beg for alms, and was located in an unhealthy area near the river. Teresa arranged for work to be done on the property and the nuns moved in on August 15, 1568. Almost immediately all of the nuns fell ill, and when Doña Maria de Mendoza, sister to the Bishop of Avila, realized how bad it was, she exchanged a far better property for the nuns' house and provided alms for their needs. On February 3, 1569, the feast of St. Blaise, the nuns went in procession to their new monastery.

Friars' first monastery in Duruelo, 1568. See F. 13-14.

Longing for a life of sacrifice to prove love

Don Rafael Mijía Veláquez

Teresa wanted to start a house for the friars and Fr. Antonio de Heredia and Fr. John of the Cross had committed themselves to start the first house. Teresa felt both were very dedicated religious and would give a good start to the work. A gentleman from Avila, Don Rafael Mijía Velázquez, offered Teresa a run-down house in a village called Duruelo. When Teresa was on her way to make the foundation in Valladolid, she stopped to see it. It was not an easy place to find and they got lost trying to. The house was adequate but very dirty. Nevertheless, the two friars wanted to begin, and Teresa felt that while she might not get permission prior to establishing the house she might if they were already living there. So, she decided to go ahead, entrusting Fr. Antonio with responsibility to provide for the house while keeping Fr. John of the Cross with her to give him instructions on the life and spirituality of the Reform. Permissions were obtained, a few essentials gathered for the house, the two friars arrived, and the first monastery of the Reform for friars officially started its new life on November 28, 1568.

When Teresa visited the house three months later, February 27, 1569, she was overjoyed at seeing the friars' simplicity, poverty, spirit of penance, and their preaching ministry to the surrounding villages. People from the area appreciated the friars' presence and brought them food and benefitted from their ministry. One of these was Don Luis de Toledo who was Lord of several nearby towns, including

Mancera de Abajo. He generously offered his support including a new property, and the friars transferred their monastery to Mancera in June 1570.

The Monastery of St. Joseph in Toledo (1569). See F. 15-16.

Insisting on the importance of poverty

An important benefactor in Toledo

While Teresa was in Valladolid involved with the foundation, she received word that an important benefactor in Toledo had died, and Teresa needed to go immediately to Toledo to deal with matters concerning a new foundation there that the benefactor had wanted to support. Teresa arrived on March 24, 1569 and stayed with Doña Luisa de la Cerda, as she had on other occasions. Negotiations for the new foundation were very complicated with the heirs of the benefactor, with the archdiocese whose bishop was under investigation by the Inquisition, and with the governor. Eventually, Teresa obtained permission but still had neither a house nor funding. She had collaborated unsuccessfully with the wealthy and powerful of the city, but it was a twenty-two year old student who eventually found a place for the nuns and helped them move in, which they did during the night because of anticipated opposition. However, in spite of their efforts, opposition still arose from neighbors and the local council, leading to threats of excommunication, but all were eventually appeased. From the start, the nuns experienced great poverty which led them to a wonderful spirit of detachment and prayer. Soon, however, benefactors came with all kinds of support, threatening to bring the spirit of poverty to an end! Knowing the benefits of poverty for progress in the spiritual life, Teresa set up the monastery in a beautiful house purchased by the original benefactor's family, but without an endowment, and agreed to them endowing the chapel as was customary in those days. Teresa was soon delighted at the depth of spiritual life in the community; the nuns gave themselves to poverty, detachment, obedience, and some to a peaceful death.

Two monasteries in Pastrana—one for nuns and the other for friars (1569). See F. 17.

Knowing nothing is achieved without struggles

Princess of Eboli and Prince Ruy Gómez

Teresa remained in Toledo for over a year, making sure the new foundation got off to a good start, especially considering the problems involved and the initial opposition. She was now grateful and peaceful that everything seemed to have worked out when she unexpectedly received a messenger from the Princess of Eboli who had previously shown interest in Teresa founding a monastery in Pastrana, asking that Teresa accompany her messenger to Pastrana where the princess awaited her. Teresa did not wish to leave Toledo, concerned that problems could still arise for the new community. However, following prayer and advice from her confessor, Teresa decided to go to Pastrana by way of Madrid. There she met some hermits who following the directives of the Council of Trent needed to identify with a religious order. After discussion with Teresa, they decided to associate themselves with Teresa's reform and since they already had a small settlement in Pastrana the second house for friars was opened once all the permissions arrived. The Princess of Eboli and her husband Prince Ruy Gómez had provided the house for the friars, and they now also provided for the nuns. The princess was very demanding and also had expectations of Teresa that were inappropriate for a religious. Once her husband died the princess wanted to enter the monastery but enclosure and the demands of religious life were too much for her and she returned to her home. She became increasingly unpleasant towards the nuns, so much so that Teresa eventually moved the monastery to Segovia.

The monastery of St. Joseph in Salamanca (1570). See F. 18-19.

Facing endless business problems

A Jesuit in Salamanca and a gentleman in the town

Teresa left Pastrana and returned to Toledo on July 22, 1569 where she finalized the purchase of a house for the local monastery. While there, she received a request from a Jesuit in Salamanca to open a house there. It would be poor and without endowment, but Teresa felt that provided the nuns were faithful to their vocation they would never be in want. On her way to Salamanca Teresa stopped in Avila and sought needed permissions. Salamanca was a university city and the house she rented would not be available until the students moved out. Moreover, she did not tell them the new renters would be nuns! Teresa set out for Salamanca with just one nun as a companion so as to maintain secrecy about the new foundation. The journey was full of hardships, but Teresa and her companion arrived on the vigil of All Saints, only to find that the students were still in the building. However, with the help of a gentleman in the town who had been keeping an eye on things for Teresa, the nuns were able to enter the house late at night. Teresa often liked to set up house and take possession of it before anyone knew what she was doing, believing that they would then be less likely to ask them to leave. In setting up this house in Salamanca, Teresa and her companion had a lot of work to do, since as Teresa puts it the students did not have the gift of cleanliness. Teresa sent for additional nuns and a local monastery of Poor Clares gave her some furnishings and alms. Eventually the monastery was in this house for about three years. As was her custom, Teresa stayed in the house until it was in a fit condition for the nuns and until the basic life of the community was running smoothly. They were renting and now bought a house hoping to move in before the next group of students wanted the rental. So, the nuns moved into their new house on the eve of the feast of St. Michael. What seemed a pleasant finalization of the new house instead was the beginning of endless problems with the owner, and three years later Teresa was still trying to sort it out. In 1579, Teresa obtained permission to move the community, and the nuns eventually moved into their new house in 1582.

The monastery of Our Lady of the Annunciation in Alba de Tormes (1571). See F. 29.

Recognizing generosity comes from well-known and unknown people

Duke of Alba and his wife

Two months following the founding of the monastery in Salamanca, the administrator of the Duke of Alba and his wife urgently requested of Teresa that she open a monastery in Alba. Once again the question arose as to how it would be funded. Teresa preferred to be without endowments, presuming the nuns could beg for alms. This became a problem when the town was too small to provide support through alms as was the case with Alba. However, the duke and his wife had desired to found a monastery for some time. The lady's confessor told her about Teresa and her new foundations, and the life and spirit of the Reform appealed to the lady. She and her husband offered to provide for a number of nuns and even moved out of their own house and into a lesser one to give the house to the new community. The foundation was made on January 25, the feast of the Conversion of St. Paul, 1571.

The monastery of St. Joseph in Segovia (1574). See F. 21,

Resolving contentious lawsuits

Doña Ana de Jimena

In 1571, Teresa was sent back to the monastery of the Incarnation as prioress. However, one day while in prayer in the monastery of Salamanca, Teresa had a vision of the Lord telling her to open a house in Segovia. Teresa realized this was not going to be easy, since the apostolic visitor, Fr. Pedro Fernádez, had made it clear to Teresa that he wanted no more foundations. However, the city and bishop supported this venture, and Fr. Fernádez surprisingly gave his consent. After previous negative experiences of buying property, Teresa decided to rent a place, set up the monastery, and then look for a suitable permanent house. Fortunately, Doña Ana de Jimena, who with her daughter later became nuns in Segovia, acquired a house and provided all that was needed. It surprised Teresa that everything moved so smoothly and the nuns entered their new monastery on the eve of the feast of St. Joseph.

Unfortunately, the bishop's permission was not in writing and the diocesan vicar general became angry, stopped the daily celebration of Mass, and removed the Blessed Sacrament. A gentleman from Alba, Antonio Gaytán, who helped Teresa with several foundations, helped with Segovia too. Eventually, the vicar general agreed to let the nuns stay but refused to allow them to have the Blessed Sacrament in the monastery. Teresa took possession of the new house on September 24, but was immediately faced with several lawsuits from the Cathedral Chapter and other religious orders, and these dragged on endlessly and required payments in settlement. So, everything started smoothly but ended only after a very contentious period. Teresa then sent for the fourteen nuns in Pastrana to come to Segovia and thus get away from the problems created by the Princess of Eboli. On September 24, 1574 the nuns moved to their new place, and then Teresa left for Avila on September 30, 1574.

Monastery of St. Joseph of the Savior in Beas (1575). See F. 22-23.

Dealing with conflicting ecclesiastical authorities

Doña Catalina and her younger sister

While Teresa was in Salamanca in 1573 a messenger arrived from Beas with letters requesting Teresa open a house and offering both a house for a monastery and a benefice for its support. Beas was a long way from the other foundations. Moreover, Teresa would have to deal yet again with the conflicting opinions and directives of Fr. General, Fr. Rubeo, who wanted more foundations and Fr. Fernandez, the apostolic commissioner, who did not want any more foundations. Teresa sought the latter's opinion and he concluded that the request should be accepted once the military order of knights who ruled the town gave approval. This sounded supportive, but Fr. Fernandez had already concluded from prior knowledge that the knights had never given permission on any previous request. Surprise! They gave permission and then Fr. Fernandez had to acquiesce. The monastery was founded on the feast of St. Matthias, 1575, with the help of two daughters of the gentleman Sancho Rodríguez de Sandoval and his wife Doña Catalina Godínez. Their elder daughter, after a period of pride and worldliness, experienced a conversion and wanted to become a nun, but her parents refused their consent. Years of suffering never weakened her resolve and after the deaths of her parents, she decided to found the monastery in Beas but obstacles were placed in the way at every turn. Eventually, the king intervened and approved the foundation and Doña Catalina and her younger sister received the habit together. Eventually, as Catalina de Jesús, she became the second prioress after Ana de Jesús for whom John of the Cross wrote the *Spiritual Canticle*, and her sister Maria de Jesús eventually became prioress of Cordoba in 1589. Both sisters had John of the Cross as their spiritual director, and he wrote three of his letters to Maria de Jesús. Both sisters suffered greatly in fidelity to their initial call and became wonderful examples of total dedication.

Monastery of St. Joseph of Carmel, Seville, 1575. See F. 24-26.

Living with the trials of travel

Teresa's brother, Lorenzo de Cepeda

While in Beas Teresa met Fr. Jerónimo Gracián who became a very important person in the development of the Reform and in Teresa's own life, and Teresa here digresses to describe his life, decision to enter Carmel, and his many virtues. At the time of their first meeting in April 1575, Fr. Gracián was superior in Andalusia, but while he was with her in Beas he received authority over all discalced friars including those in Castile.

Teresa had been working on a possible foundation in Caravaca but permission included the monastery's subjection to the military order of knights, and Teresa would not agree to that. So, the Caravaca foundation was delayed until Teresa could get the king to intervene on her behalf. Since both Caravaca and Beas were in the ecclesiastical province of Andalusia, Fr. Gracián who was responsible for that region understood the problems Teresa faced. So, in the meantime, Teresa turned her thoughts to Seville where wealthy people had already indicated they would provide a house, and the archbishop was in favor of the foundation. So, Teresa sent the prioress and nuns who had been destined for Caravaca to Seville instead. Teresa accompanied the group, journeying in intense heat, arriving on May 26, 1575, after many trials, sickness, unpleasant accommodations, and a break-away barge that took everyone's strength and a little luck to control it.

The second day after Pentecost, they reached Cordoba, but were held up because they had to get a magistrate's permission to cross the river, and when they received it their wagons were unfortunately too wide to cross the bridge. Teresa hoped to arrive in secret as she usually did, but found the church packed for a local celebration and the congregation's reaction to the nuns was overwhelmingly positive.

On arriving in Seville, things were not as Teresa expected. The archbishop's permission had been presumed but not obtained in writing. He told them he was against founding new monasteries without endowments, and Teresa wanted her monasteries to be founded in poverty—the only exceptions were monasteries in towns too small to give opportunity for alms. After a lot of misunderstanding, pain, and lack of funds even for basic needs, the archbishop gave his support and the community was started in a rented house.

Seville was not supportive of foundations; Teresa received a little help and insufficient alms, women who said they would join the community then thought her Reform too strict, and the experience was different than Teresa had seen elsewhere. In the midst of this unsatisfactory situation, Teresa was called to Castile as a result of misunderstandings that resulted in the General Chapter of Piacenza's banning any further foundations and even imposing a kind of self-imprisonment on Teresa. Just before her departure, her brother, Lorenzo de Cepeda, returned from the Indies and began to help Teresa find a house for the community. He, together with a generous gentleman, Garciálvarez, arranged a contract in a few days. However, further problems arose—the occupant did not want to leave and a nearby Franciscan community did everything to dissuade the nuns from setting up their new community. Again, Teresa entered by night. More problems arose, this time concerning clauses in the contract. However, the nuns received aid from one or two generous people, and Teresa's brother worked on some restructuring of the house. In June, 1576, there was a great celebration. The streets were decorated and all kinds of groups participated as the archbishop brought the Blessed Sacrament in procession to the community's new house—Sunday before Pentecost, 1576. Teresa left the next day.

St. Joseph's Caravaca (1576). See F. 27.

Balancing jurisdictional dependence and independence

Doña Catalina de Otalora and three young ladies

The foundation in Caravaca was due to the initiative of Doña Catalina de Otalora and three young ladies. When Teresa went to Beas in 1575 she took with her sufficient numbers of nuns for two monasteries—Beas and Caravaca. However, both places were under the jurisdiction of the regional military order of knights who insisted in the contract that obedience be given to them. Teresa rejected this, and for the time being the foundation in Caravaca was put on hold and the extra nuns were sent to Seville instead. The ladies who had asked Teresa to start the foundation lived as in an enclosure and, once a new permission was given by the king without subjection to the knights, nuns were sent from Malagón and the monastery was founded on the feast of the Holy Name of Jesus in 1576. Teresa was not present for the opening since she was still in Seville.

Villanueva de la Jara (1580). See F. 28.

Merging communities with different spiritualities

Town council, nine dedicated women

Teresa left Seville in 1576 and went to Toledo. While there, changes in Papal Nuncio, delegates, and counselors led to the persecution of the discalced friars and attempts to undermine the Reform. Interventions by the king and by Fr. Pedro Fernandez and the support of many noblemen and bishops helped alleviate the trials. Around this time a priest from Villanueva de la Jara came with letters from the town council asking Teresa to accept as a monastery a shrine with a little house attached where nine women lived an intense spiritual life. Teresa wanted to reject the request for several reasons—too many women to merge with a new community, no funding, no adequate house, and too far away from other monasteries of the Reform. Having discussed this with her confessor, Teresa sent a non-committal response. Entreaties continued for four years, together with the support of leading friars and promises of financial support. Teresa replied with further reasons for not accepting this offer. After another month or so, Teresa received letters from the town council offering to provide for the needs of the monastery and from other leading people offering enthusiastic support. Teresa still resisted, concerned especially that the nine local sisters would overwhelm the spirit of the new community with their own values rather than those of the Carmelite Reform.

While in prayer the Lord spoke to Teresa, telling her not to hesitate to accept this house. So, Teresa went personally with four nuns, two from Toledo and two from Malagón. Just outside the town Teresa and her little group stopped at the friars' monastery of Our Lady of Succor to inform the town of their arrival. They entered Villanueva de la Jara on February 21, the first Sunday of Lent, 1580, received by the city council, important people in the area, and members from other religious orders. The procession was splendid, as the Blessed Sacrament was carried to the church. When Teresa met the nine women who lived there she was overjoyed at the spirituality, poverty, penance, and prayer, and they too welcomed the small group of nuns who had come to form a community with them. The former had suffered for years in their efforts to found a monastery. Once the joined community was set up there were some initial conflicts as Teresa had expected but the quality of the nuns lives enabled them to come together and the house flourished.

St. Joseph of Our Lady of the Street, Palencia (1580). See F. 29.

Rejoicing in the Lord's guidance

Canon Reinosa

Don Alonso de Mendoza, former Bishop of Avila, a strong supporter of Teresa, and since June 1577 Bishop of Palencia, sent word to Teresa that he wanted her to found a monastery in his diocese. At the time, Teresa was very ill and also not inclined to start a monastery in Palencia because it would be without endowment—which Teresa preferred, but neither did it have sufficient hope of support from alms since the city was poor. Teresa stopped at Valladolid on the way to Palencia, and while she had thought about foundations in Palencia and Burgos she seemed to have no energy or confidence to move ahead on either of them. Teresa received some encouragement from Fr. Ripalda and the Jesuit provincial. One day after Communion the Lord spoke to Teresa, "What do you fear? When have I failed you?" Teresa began at once to make arrangements and she took two nuns with her, and planned to buy a house in Palencia. Although, as Teresa expected, Palencia did not offer adequate opportunities for alms, a gentleman offered temporary use of his house. Teresa asked that the gentleman vacate the house secretly and not to tell anyone who was coming. She wrote to a canon of the city whom she did not know but heard he was a servant of God and asked for his help. Canon Reinosa did a great job providing the house with supplies and beds and Teresa and her nuns arrived before anyone was aware of their presence—a new foundation on the feast of King David, December 29, 1580. The bishop came and joined in the rejoicing.

Settled into the rental house, Teresa began looking for a more permanent residence, and the bishop suggested two buildings near a shrine to Our Lady of the Street. The cathedral chapter and local confraternity made a gift of the shrine but the owners of the houses, seeing the interest, increased the price. However, Teresa did not think the houses suitable and Canon Reinosa and another canon looked around for a better set-up. However, Teresa was guided by the Lord to buy the first houses with all their problems since she saw it was the Lord's will. Moreover, it was in a bad part of town and the nuns' presence drove evil away. Once the contract was signed with the diocesan administrator as guarantor, there followed the official opening. On May 26th, 1581, the bishop led a solemn procession.

Monastery of the Blessed Trinity, Soria (1581). See F. 30.

Celebrating welcome and enthusiasm

Bishop Velázquez, Doña Beatriz de Beamonte y Navarra

Bishop Alonso Velázquez, a former confessor of Teresa and then the bishop of Osma wrote to Teresa from Soria, telling her that a generous and spiritually dedicated woman he knew, Doña Beatriz de Beamonte y Navarra, wanted to start a foundation in Soria. She offered a house and a very generous endowment, and the bishop offered a very fine church that could easily be connected to the monastery. Teresa agreed, chose seven nuns, and the bishop sent a coach for them and his delegate arranged a pleasant trip and good accommodation. The group arrived at El Burgo de Osma on May 31, 1581 and Soria the next day. The lady whose house it was had prepared it really well for the nuns, and the only thing they needed was the construction of the passageway to the church. Doña Beatriz and Bishop Velázquez were wonderful collaborators for this foundation. Teresa left Soria on August 16, but the trip to Avila was nowhere near as pleasant as that to Soria; the roads were bad, the wagon overturned, and the guides abandoned them. They stopped at Segovia on August 23, and while the journey had been terrible, Teresa rejoiced at the peace and support of the new foundation in Palencia.

St. Joseph of St. Anne, Burgos, 1582. See F. 31.

Struggling with bishops' support and opposition

Doña Catalina de Tolosa

Over the course of six years, several Jesuits had urged Teresa to open a house in Burgos. Teresa met the new archbishop of Burgos when he passed through Valladolid on his way to enter his new diocese. Teresa asked Don Alvaro de Mendoza to intercede with the new archbishop, seeking permission to open a house in Burgos. In fact, the archbishop was well-aware of Teresa's work and very supportive. He wrote to Teresa expressing his support and urged her to visit Burgos and discuss the matter with the council. However, he told her that with or without the council's support he would go ahead and approve it. However, Teresa needed the council's support to assure the financial well-being of the foundation. Moreover, Teresa had an uncomfortable feeling that the archbishop might not be as supportive as he claimed. She decided to put the request aside and go to Avila.

However, a widow of Burgos, Doña Catalina de Tolosa, who had sent four of her daughters to Teresa's convents, had been looking for a house in Burgos for the new foundation and was already getting things they would need. She even consulted important people in the town and got a magistrate to submit a request to the council for permission to open a foundation and they granted it. In November, letters arrived indicating the license had been granted and urging Teresa to go at once to Burgos—they had a house and the needed funding. The trip to Burgos was terrible, the weather appalling, the guides inexperienced, and the river-crossing frightening. The group arrived in late January and were enthusiastically welcomed by friends, well-wishers, and the city council.

However, things changed the next day when the provincial, Fr. Gracián, visited the archbishop who was very angry, especially at Teresa for having gone ahead without his written approval. He even suggested the nuns could return from where they came! Eventually, the archbishop allowed temporary residence until the nuns had adequate income but his administrator created all kinds of problems and placed obstacles in the way of starting the foundation in Doña Catalina's house and in approving guarantors for the purchase of a permanent place. A temporary solution was to have a few rooms in a nearby hospital which also had a chapel the nuns could use. Eventually, with the aid of a friend of Fr. Gracián's, a house was found and the archbishop rejoiced, but when the nuns moved in he became angry again and a new set of endless problems arose. Teresa asked Bp. Velázquez to help pacify the archbishop. On April 18, 1582, the archbishop gave the required license. After a long and very painful process the foundation of Burgos was realized and the archbishop eventually became a supporter of the monastery and begged forgiveness for the way he had treated the nuns.

A short treatise on prayer and other counsels (chaps. 4-8; 18. 6-13)

In these chapters Teresa is concerned to promote spiritual development and the life of prayer and to give guidance in assuring the experiences are authentic. *Some may well be afraid to undertake the spiritual journey* and while there are always dangers and risks in this journey there are greater risks in not pursuing it. We must proceed with courage and humility, entrusting ourselves to the compassionate love of God. The nuns in the early foundations exemplified the qualities needed to undertake this spiritual journey; namely, firm desire, detachment, and fidelity to the original charism and traditions.

It is important in the life of prayer not to focus too much on intellectual concentration—trying to think and meditate without distractions. Not everyone can concentrate all the time without distractions. In any case love is more important than intellectual concentration. The soul is not the mind, nor is thinking the object of the will. *Progress does not lie in thinking much, but in loving much.* Sometimes thinking about what we owe God and of who God is and who we are can be helpful for beginners. However, the object of the spiritual journey is the acquisition of love, seen in obedience to the will of God and in the service of our neighbors. These two components of our love must take precedence over any satisfactions we may gain from thinking and meditating on God and enjoying the blessings God gives us. When these satisfactions are no longer present we might become displeased and dissatisfied, but this reaction is often a form of self-love and false security.

True love of the Lord makes one restless for the good of others in actions and in prayer, leaving aside all interest in self-satisfaction in order to pursue obedience to the Lord's will. We must live in the real world, at times with lots of responsibilities, and we might think that spiritual growth is not possible when immersed in so many distractions. But let us keep clear priorities; if we are determined to love, we must do God's will and fulfill our responsibilities. If we do, we will be amazed at the spiritual growth we find in ourselves. We all know people who dutifully respond to all their obligations, whether in daily work, government, and so on, and they never seem to have a day to themselves or adequate times for prayer. Such people do much good to others, and the Lord blesses them with true liberty of spirit. In desiring nothing they possess all; they live in peace for they depend on and obey God alone. So, let us not be discouraged when duties of obedience or charity call us away from the solitude we might prefer.

The greatest development in spiritual life comes from obedience to the will of God and not from the delights of the mystical life. We should never seek to please ourselves but only to please the one we love. We can often deceive ourselves into thinking withdrawal from duties and from the service of others into times of aloneness will be better; but fulfilling God's will is more important. We can always deceive ourselves with "good" reasons to be alone. We must surrender ourselves in obedience to God's will, with all the sacrifices and struggles that love demands. So, if we must leave the pleasures of solitude in obedience to God's will, we will dispose ourselves better for spiritual union rather than pursuing some mystical absorption that leads to self-love. Some may suggest that in solitude there are fewer occasions to offend the Lord than in all the interactions or distractions that present themselves in daily obligations and duties. But true love is not gained by hiding or escaping, but in the midst of occasions of falling. Surely, solitude is the best choice, but when daily duties call us away we can prove our love, patience, and humility. Being in the midst of occasions of failure also helps us gain self-knowledge, appreciate the value of time for the Lord and be grateful for a new understanding of prayer. Quality prayer does not depend on the time given but on the intensity of love and involvement in duties, and good works help kindle this love.

Teresa expressed *concern about false mystical experiences.* Throughout her writings she explains genuine spiritual and mystical stages in prayer and their effects, even physical ones. However, in this section she speaks about harm that comes to spiritual persons who do not know when to resist experiences that they think are good but that Teresa considers harmful. Some people experience a spiritual absorption (see F. 6. 3f) that seems similar to an ecstasy or rapture that she refers to elsewhere in her writings. However, the latter comes from God, is generally short-lived, and a person is helpless to do anything about it. The absorption Teresa is concerned about starts like the prayer of quiet and resembles a spiritual sleep but lasts for seven to eight hours and seems to be prolonged by the recipient who cannot let go of the delight he or she feels. People who have these experiences and allow them to progress can be deceived into thinking they are genuine ecstasy. However, this absorption concerns the pleasurable and is not centered on prayer as a relationship with the person of God. This absorbing concentration may be focused on God or on some other matter. The inability to break out of this absorption is a weakness that can result from a person's nature, health, depression, and so on, and especially from an unwillingness to give up the satisfaction he or she feels in these experiences. In genuine ecstasy the faculties are passive, but in this false version they remain deliriously active. This absorption has none of the benefits of authentic ecstasy. In fact, it is a bodily weakness. In these cases a person should think about something else or get involved in a distracting but useful task. Teresa also condemns the excessive participation in Communion, either because of the pleasant satisfaction it gives, or as a remedy for absorption, or from an impulse of desire for union with the Lord. These and other false ecstasies that control us and leave our reason without freedom should be considered suspect. As a rule, if the emphasis is on sensible delight in these spiritual experiences, a person should seek to stop them.

A difficulty that Teresa had seen in her communities arose from what she calls *the problem of "melancholy,"* which seems to be a catchall term for various forms of mental sickness—real or imaginary (F. 7). Perhaps our terms "depression" or "neurosis" would cover much of its meaning but not all. Certainly this illness causes problems for the individual but also for the community and for those in positions of responsibility. There are greater and lesser degrees of this illness, in some cases the afflicted person causes no harm to others and can be helped in the early stages. However, some seem to use this situation to get their own way and thus disrupt the community. Teresa believes that in many sufferers their reason is diminished and they seem out of control, and so insists that healthy responses must always include rational arguments and actions. Teresa also is convinced that temporary or prolonged confinement can help, for she feels that some are overpowered by their own interests, and this can lead to their spiritual well-being falling into danger.

Some know they are ill and bear this burden. They humbly follow directions, entrusting themselves obediently to others. They live a martyrdom. Others become manipulative, and some who are not ill begin to act as if they are and expect everyone else to put up with them. Either case brings havoc to the community. Teresa is firm in telling superiors not to tolerate anyone who takes liberties in community for they can thus bring harm to others. She feels that many who claim to be melancholic lack humility, self-discipline, and obedience. It is interesting that Teresa feels the term "melancholy" is overused, and she would prefer not to hear it used in her communities. It often seems a cover-up for self-will, unhealthy freedom, and is often used as a defense for unacceptable behavior. In some cases medicine will be required and time in the infirmary. When treatment is made available, a person in such situations must understand that his or her behavior must change. A superior should show lots of love and understanding, when necessary keep the patient occupied and distracted, and even limit times of prayer when the imagination can get out of control. People with this affliction often do not want to acknowledge that they have it, since it is not like other illnesses that require bed-rest and a doctor. With other illnesses one can be cured or die, but this one drags on endlessly bringing afflictions, fantasies, and scruples—which the sick person thinks are temptations when, in fact, they are the result of this sickness. Everyone will need compassion in dealing with this problem.

The Lord leads some along the path of revelations and visions. This is a fact, even though many confessors and directors are afraid of such experiences. They seem open to the idea of a devil tempting us but not God giving revelations and visions! However, *there are times when the revelations and visions are false*—but a person with humility will not be deceived. One's reactions to visions must always be accompanied by humility. Good or evil does not lie in a vision but in the person who sees it, and whether or not he or she benefits in humility. People who receive visions should not think they are saints or have earned the visions by their good deeds—that is pride. Rather they should focus on their unworthiness and need of sacrifice, prayer, and commitment not to offend the Lord. In the case of revelations one should discuss the matter with a learned director and seek his or her guidance so that together they can discern the object of the revelation. This is important since some people can deceive themselves and imagine visions. It is always appropriate to wait a while to see if the revelations come to pass. It is also necessary to know the temperament and virtue of a person claiming revelations and when necessary seek advice from someone learned and experienced in these matters. Moreover, whatever the source of these experiences one must be prudent not to talk about them to others, but maintain oneself in humility, obedience, and a spirit of sacrifice.

Discretion is important for anyone who leads others in the spiritual life. Teresa insists that superiors and directors should not expect others to be like themselves. What one finds easy another does not. Sometimes one reduces everything in the spiritual life to prayer, but others move along a different path. Some give themselves to a lot of mortification and think everyone else should do the same. Rather, a superior should be attentive to each one's talents and ways of spiritual development. A superior cannot make someone perfect by force, but should allow each one to proceed gradually in following the Lord. Likewise, the superior should be careful regarding the demands she puts on others under obedience, since some can take things too literally and even get themselves in difficulties (F. 18. 7). Those in authority can learn much in the guidance of others from contact with people who are learned in the spiritual life.

A few final thoughts from Teresa

- Many of the good people you meet in life are placed in your path by a loving God.
- Some people seem dedicated to impeding what you think needs to be done, but with hindsight you might find they were correct.
- Things pertaining to prayer and spiritual growth are often discredited in our modern world, make sure this does not prevent you from undertaking this journey.
- Do not be sad when you need to be involved in external matters because of your duties and responsibilities, for this is a sure way to union with God's will.
- Love is seen not in hiding in corners but in the midst of the occasions of falling; you must prove love in the real world.
- You achieve nothing without struggles.
- Poverty brings you assurance that all is on solid foundations.

Chapter Eight

Some other writings of St. Teresa

In Teresa's day women did not write serious works on any subject; that was part of a man's world! It was especially unthinkable that a woman would write about theological issues. Up to the twelfth century that was the task of monks in their monasteries, to give a deeper spiritual interpretation to the literal understandings of Scripture. Then, in the twelfth and thirteenth centuries the task of writing about theological matters passed to theologians to work out responses to each disputed question. In a particular way women did not write about their own spiritual experiences, since no one really cared, and some considered they were probably inauthentic! There are only a handful of Spanish women writers in the fourteenth to fifteenth centuries, among them Leonor López de Cordoba who wrote her memoirs of life at court and linked them to devotion to the Virgin Mary. Then there was the fifteenth century poet, Florencia del Pinar, who wrote of love, including sensual love, which was unusual for that time.

We have seen that Teresa had no preparations as a writer. She was forty five years old when she wrote her first spiritual testimony in 1560 and would continue to write for twenty two years until the year before her death in 1582. We have seen that Teresa often wrote because one superior-confessor or another imposed the obligation on her in view of her vow of obedience. However, there are other writings, both prose and poetry, that Teresa freely writes, many of which she clearly intended to share with others. Teresa does not correct or edit most of her works, but a few do undergo reviews and these lead in some cases to rewrites.

As we have seen, Teresa's four major works are the *Autobiography* (1565), the *Way of Perfection* (1566), the *Interior Castle* (1577), and the *Foundations* (1573-1582). She also wrote sixty five *Spiritual Testimonies*, seventeen *Soliloquies* or prayerful exclamations, seven chapters of reflections on the *Song of Songs*, two spiritual challenges, the Constitutions, advice "On Making the Visitation," and thirty one poems. The largest collection of her writings is her letters. Fr. Tomás Alvarez identifies 468, and some authors think Teresa may have written as many as 25,000. In this chapter we deal with a selection of Teresa's other writings to give readers a taste of the wealth of spiritual insights Teresa offers us. Many of Teresa's followers rarely read the "secondary" works and miss so much of her prayer life and spiritual challenges. So, hopefully, these summaries may become an introduction to some of Teresa's works beyond the four great major ones. Since there are many components to each writing, readers may well choose to just reflect on one point each day as a meditation on these key elements in Teresa's teachings and in the stages of the spiritual life.

Prior to the twentieth century, women rarely represented their lives in print. Teresa did! (Teresa authorized the publication of the Way of Perfection in Portugal). Women in Teresa's time, especially nuns, rarely posed for portraits. Teresa did! (In 1576 Teresa posed for Juan de la Miseria, a young Italian painter. Teresa was 61 at the time). "Representation thus serves to define the relative value of male and female, or gender relationship."[11] Indirectly, whether she intended it or not, Teresa is establishing female authority in a world where women were deprived of all relevant authority.

Spiritual Testimonies (In some editions "Relations")

The sixty five *Spiritual Testimonies* give snapshots of Teresa's spiritual life. Some are lengthy explanations of her state of soul at various stages in her life. Others are very short—a few lines—and give an insight into one or other aspect of her spiritual life, or guidance for others, or needed virtues, and so on. Some of the spiritual testimonies describe Teresa's state of soul, often in response to confessors' requests. Thus, *Spiritual Testimonies* 1-3 are written for Fr. Ibáñez and Fr. García de Toledo. The first spiritual testimony predates the *Autobiography* but is after Teresa's encounter with St. Peter of Alcántara in 1559 and the subsequent double charism of understanding and communication—which are in addition to her original charism of mystical experience. Given this is Teresa's first attempt to write about her spiritual life, it is an extraordinary presentation of the nature of recollection, of the blessings and pains that come with impulses of love, of the intensity of anxious longings, of the prayer of quiet and its consequences, of the pains of living in this world while longing for the next, and of profound gratitude to the Lord for his transforming gifts. In a second spiritual testimony to Fr. Ibáñez (1565) and a third to Fr. García de Toledo she explains progress she has made in deeper visions and revelations but also speaks about her own responses in poverty, compassion, and bearing trials. She has increased self-knowledge, perseverance in spite of trials, courage, calmness, and a desire to accept sufferings. These first three testimonies set the scene for the *Autobiography* which she writes in 1562 and 1565.

In 1576 when Teresa is already in the final stage of the mystical life, she writes another testimony on the state of her soul, written for Fr. Rodrigo Alvarez who was Teresa's spiritual director, but here in his capacity as consultant to the Spanish Inquisition in Seville (ST 58). Teresa had been accused of illuminism and instructed to respond in writing. While the Inquisition was interested in Teresa's unusual mystical experiences, she sets the scene by insisting her interests have always been on the mysteries and passion of the Lord with no desire for anything else. In fact, she points out her faithfulness to her obligations in spite of twenty two years of aridity in her spiritual life and devotions. However, eighteen years before writing this spiritual testimony she began to experience a series of revelations, locutions, and visions. These disturbed her as she was unsure of their source, and so over a period of six years she spoke to lots of learned and spiritually experienced persons to seek their counsel—Teresa speaks of twenty by name and mentions several unnamed others. This was a trying time for Teresa, filled with embarrassment and misunderstanding, but she insisted her purpose in these discussions was to be faithful to the Church's teachings. Thus, she submitted all her life and experiences to her confessors in obedience, humility, and faith. Since others heard of her experiences, she had to deal with persecutions and fear and did so with joy, humility, a spirit of poverty, and solitude. Teresa clarifies that her visions were intellectual not imaginative, at times ecstatic, and often consoling for her in her afflictions and persecutions. They were not continual but came when there was some need. In all cases she focused not on the visions but on her sins, and excelled in obedience to her confessors.

The same year Teresa wrote the above spiritual testimony for Fr. Rodrigo Alvarez in his capacity as consultant to the Inquisition, she also wrote to him a second testimony on the degrees of contemplative prayer in his capacity as her spiritual director (ST 59). Teresa submits her presentation to Fr. Alvarez's critique but insists she has experienced these stages of prayer. The first degree of contemplative prayer which follows a constant awareness of the presence of God is interior recollection in which a person focuses exclusively on communion with God in solitude. This leads to a prayer of interior quiet and peace when a person wants nothing but to love God. There follows the sleep of the faculties in which the will is passive to all but God while the intellect and imagination continue their normal functions. Union happens when all faculties are completely passive; the will loves, the intellect is in awe at the love, and there is no memory at all— for all are in union with God. These experiences of union pass quickly but move on to ecstasy in which the suspension of all faculties last longer and is even felt exteriorly as if the body freezes up. Teresa tells us that this is a time of rejoicing and of revelation that leaves one with an awareness of one's misery and ingratitude.

Beyond the ecstatic suspension, a person experiences in the intimate depths of his or her being a revelation of divine knowledge that transports a person to a new level of being, and then surrenders to the Lord to be taken away to higher levels. This experience produces strong virtues, repentance for past faults, and a longing that God always be praised. At times there arises a flight of the spirit, like a fire that suddenly bursts into flame, and one escapes from the body and rises up to go wherever the Lord wills. Sometimes a person's painful longing for God gives rise to an impulse of love. Everything brings pain and in this solitude and abandonment one yearns for death in order to be in union with God. When God gives glimpses of the future union the soul's desire and longing increase. A further type of prayer is when a person feels he or she has been wounded with an arrow of love in the depths of his or her spirit. The wound causes pain but produces transformations in the depths of one's spirit. Teresa concludes that all these are real experiences and not imagined, and when they pass the soul knows they have passed. All these experiences lead to union with the Trinity.

Teresa's final statement on the state of her spiritual life was written in 1581 for her former confessor, Bishop Alonso Velásquez, at the time Bishop of Osma. Teresa is completely at peace, lives with security, and feels confirmed in the Lord's graces. She is full of gratitude for what she recognizes as unmerited gifts of God. She remains forgetful of self and directs her entire being to the glory of God and the fulfillment of God's will. Previous imaginative visions are no more, and Teresa now continues to enjoy intellectual visions of the Trinity and the humanity of Christ, along with interior locutions that guide her. Acts, feelings, and commitments that were important in the past no longer are. She is at peace, detached from everything except the love and the will of God. She lives in the presence of the Trinity, desiring neither death nor life, but totally surrendered to God's will and to the desire to love God.

> Two of the Spiritual Testimonies include explicit commands from the Lord to write down the advice he gives both for her own benefit (ST 24: "Don't forget to write down the counsels I give you, so that you don't forget them") or for the benefit of others (ST 48: ". . . don't' neglect to write down what I say; for even though it may not benefit you, it can benefit others"). So, in response to these commands Teresa writes down these extraordinary testimonies.

Among the spiritual testimonies there are a series that reveal elements of the nature and development of the spiritual life. The pursuit of union with God does not consist in just being close to God nor in receiving spiritual favors, but in being detached from everything that is not in conformity with God's will (ST 25). There are many objects that help us in our spiritual journey, and we should not with a false sense of poverty renounce them if they awaken love (ST 26). This love became so great for Teresa that she experienced being drawn into spiritual marriage with the Lord, called to mutual love and union (ST 31). This marriage means sharing everything, including friendship and also trials, pains, and suffering (ST 46). The Lord confirms this marriage by placing a precious ring on Teresa's hand (ST 34). Working, suffering, loving are all part of the journey of love. The journey is filled with trials, aridity, and loneliness, for suffering is the way of truth in life (ST 32). Then all our actions show forth the commitment of our will in surrender to God (ST 47) and in our dedication to good works.

This spiritual journey leads to infused knowledge of the Trinity and to a vital experience of their union and interrelationship (ST 42). Teresa understands that the Trinity is in the soul by presence, power, and essence, for we are made in the image of God (ST 49).

Throughout her spiritual journey Teresa receives constant guidance from the Lord (ST 7), on topics such as the role of public ecstasies (ST 9) and the importance of Teresa's work of new foundations even when this meant leaving the enclosure (ST 15). Then, too, the Lord guides her in her ministry and work of reform, telling Teresa that new houses would give opportunity for many to serve God. At times the Lord gives Teresa specific advice on organization and new foundations (ST 6), assuring her that the order of the Blessed Virgin would flourish (ST 11), and specifically that St. Joseph's would be recognized as a holy foundation (ST 18), and that the Incarnation would evidence spiritual improvement (ST 27). The Lord confirms Teresa in her mission to reform Carmel (ST 30, 33), even giving specific advice regarding particular monasteries (ST 45). While in Seville in 1575, Teresa had a vision in which the Lord told her to establish a special feast in honor of his Mother, Our Lady (ST 39), and later in the same city a clarification that God's law takes precedence over all else (ST 41). When people threatened to suppress the Reform, the Lord assured Teresa they would not succeed (ST 57).

At times, Teresa's spiritual testimonies deal with certain virtues necessary for spiritual growth. The Lord tells Teresa that detachment from this world's values is important for God's standards are different than the world's (ST 5). Teresa learns that provided one has the right intentions, involvement in daily business affairs does not impede this (ST 8); the key need is obedience to God's will—that is better than penance (ST 19). Above all one must have humility in the spiritual life for one achieves nothing without God's grace. True humility is knowing what one can do and what God can do (ST 24). This leads to total surrender but also to joy in appreciating all that God has given (ST 10).

Now and again, Teresa's visions that lead to spiritual testimonies deal with family and friends. Thus, she prays for her brother (ST 16), and makes a vow to Fr. Gracían (ST 35). The Lord confirms this latter with a vision in which the two are joined together (ST 36) and assures Teresa that Fr. Gracían was his gift to her. Teresa, after some struggles, vows to obey Gracían for the rest of her life. Teresa felt this was not restrictive but actually brought her great freedom and blessings from the Lord (ST 38). Later, in a vision, the Lord assures Teresa of the health of Gracían (ST 50) and of his consoling presence (ST 54).

Teresa's own spiritual life is profoundly enriched by a series of visions that she shares with us in her spiritual testimonies. Of special note are four intellectual visions of the indwelling of the Holy Trinity. Teresa sees the Three Persons as One and yet each as distinct, so much so that each one offers her a gift; one offers love, a second offers love outpoured in the ability to suffer, and the third offers the enkindling of love. This experience brings Teresa great delight and great awareness of her sinfulness (ST 13). Teresa continues to have a habitual experience of the indwelling of the Trinity within her, and while she had difficulty in understanding three in one, the Lord tells her that on a spiritual level there are different ways of thinking and understanding. Teresa sees the Trinity communicating with the entire world, while also communicating directly with her (ST 14). Yet again in an intellectual vision she receives infused knowledge of the Holy Trinity (ST 29). On another occasion, God shows Teresa what a soul is like when in the company of the Holy Trinity, filled with power over the whole world, and also how helpless and bound is a person in sin (ST 20). Besides these visions of the Trinity, Teresa also had a vision of our Lady presiding over the monastery of the Incarnation in the prioress' place (ST 21).

Many of Teresa's visions show how the Lord is always close to her, guiding her, challenging her, and giving her signs of his love. When in Seville in 1575, Teresa had an intellectual vision that showed her how close the Lord was to her. This came at a time of fear, persecution, and suffering that plagued Teresa for a few days. The Lord appears close to her, challenging her to understand how helpless she is without him, and consoling her with assurances of his nearness and of the Father's union with her. This lasted about a month (ST 53). Three years earlier, while in Avila, Teresa had an intimate experience of the Lord's Eucharistic presence in which he reminded her that he shed his blood for her. This culminated several days of suffering in which Teresa could not eat, but the Lord appeared to her and broke bread for her to eat, another sign of his consoling presence (ST 22). These Eucharistic encounters led to much progress for Teresa in her spiritual life.

Soliloquies (In some editions "Exclamations")

According to Luis de León these personal prayerful exclamations were written by St. Teresa following a series of experiences she had after communion on various days in 1569 when she was in the sixth mansion, a period of ecstatic prayer. In all her writings Teresa frequently digresses to spontaneously express her prayer to God. These seventeen prayerful reflections give us insight into Teresa's devotion, and we are allowed to listen to her personal prayer and share in her self-gift to God.

Throughout this book on the *Contemporary Challenge of St. Teresa of Avila* I have given summaries of her writings to enable readers to gain overviews of her works in a relatively short time and space. Of course, it is always better to read directly Teresa's own works, listen to her voice, and respond to her challenges. Summaries are helpful but they can never catch the spirit of Teresa's own words. It is particularly difficult to summarize her own prayers for we lose the spirit, intimacy, wonder, and spontaneity of her prayer.

Soliloquy 1. Teresa cries in pain at being separated from God. She sees how useless her life is when spent away from her Lord, and exclaims that all she wants to do is to serve the Lord. She tells us that when she is in God's presence, God achieves everything in her, and she wants never to be an obstacle to God's actions within her. She knows God is always attentive to her, and she cries in hope of never being separated from her Lord.

Soliloquy 2. In yearning to be with God Teresa exclaims how she has learnt to value the quiet of solitude, where she can avoid the painful distractions of the world around her. But even solitude can be painful as one appreciates that one is not united fully with the Lord and misses him so much. In this world's solitude one is alone, but in solitude with God one learns to love and longs to serve and reach out to others.

Teresa asks would it not be better to leave all others to be alone with God and concludes it is better to love the Lord by learning to love others for his sake. She sees and experiences that genuine solitude must always be linked to serving others.

Soliloquy 3. Teresa shares how sad she feels that God's immense love receives so little gratitude; in fact how people live, sometimes in sin, forgetting God's enduring love for them. Teresa expresses her gratitude to the merciful Redeemer who continues to love us with tenderness in spite of our forgetfulness. Teresa cries out against the hard of heart, ungrateful, and unresponsive, and she prays God will change the misdirection of so many lives before it is too late. Teresa praises God's enduring love, and blesses the Lord who sacrifices himself for the world's salvation and fills all with his merciful love.

Soliloquy 4. Teresa delights in thinking about eternal life with God but laments over so many lost opportunities and wasted time in this life. Fortunately God's mercy and magnificent works never end, and God can recover and make good our lost opportunities. Teresa praises God's transforming greatness and power.

Soliloquy 5. When we have been so unreliable how can we ask God for more favors? Teresa stresses how much we depend on God's healing aid and how we should always petition God for everything we need. In the gospel Martha was concerned that the Lord did not seem interested in her needs and she dared complain. But the Lord showed her how love alone gives value to everything. We cannot give this love unless God first gives it to us. So, Teresa asks God to give to her what she wants to give back to God—a love in conformity with God's will.

Soliloquy 6. Teresa, dissatisfied with this life, asks how long she must wait before seeing God. She feels wounded with a painful longing for she desires nothing but to love God. She finds no remedy for her painful longings. However, above all she gives herself to God's will.

Soliloquy 7. Teresa rejoices to know God delights to be with all men and women, even sinners or those with little faith. How extraordinary is God's loving mercy towards us. The Trinity who shares love with each other also shares that love with us and asks that we return our love to God. Teresa rejoices that in the Son love is returned to the Father. In and through the Son we can join our love and praise God as God deserves.

Soliloquy 8. Teresa celebrates that in the Lord we find the words of eternal life and asks God to use divine power that she never withdraws from these words. The Lord tells us that when we are burdened he will give us consolation and rest. So many people remain unhappy because they do not seek their rest in God. Teresa asks God to cure people's blindness so they can see God's assuring Word and comforting rest. God loves those who do not love in return, or heals those who love their sickness. May God's goodness and mercy help us.

Soliloquy 9. We burn up in our sins and need the living water that only God can provide. God gives us an unfailing promise to always provide life-giving water to quench our needs. Teresa prays that God quench the thirst of those who do not recognize their need and have no pity for themselves in their misfortunes. Teresa tells God how much she needs this water and pleads God will always put out fires, heal her wounds, and give life to her soul.

Soliloquy 10. We offend and expect forgiveness; we seem to remember God's great mercy and forget that justice is also a reality. Everywhere we forget how much God is hurt by our endless sin. Even as friends we let God down and betray this compassionate love. Teresa pleads that God help her bring her own failures to an end and also to raise up those who do not seem to want to be raised up. May God's boundless compassion remove the hardness of human hearts.

Soliloquy 11. Teresa cries out as she thinks of the endless torment of those who have rejected God and have chosen eternal separation, eternal torment, and to be surrounded by a pitiless company of fellow sufferers. Why are people blind and deaf to the future that awaits them? Teresa prays for these souls that they will see and understand through the merits of the Son.

Soliloquy 12. Teresa laments how so many people withdraw themselves from God's love. They are sick, blind, and mad, as they turn all their fury against God. They have no strength to withstand occasions of sin but use all their strength to oppose God and divine love and turn to live in darkness. What blindness, what ingratitude! Teresa prays that God's enduring compassion may provide a remedy. Teresa appeals that these treacherous souls end their wickedness and return to God's love. May they appreciate God's love or at least divine judgment.

Soliloquy 13. Teresa speaks to the communion of saints asking that they be intercessors, helping us in our misery, pleading for divine mercy, sharing their understanding, and telling us of the joy they now experience. Unfortunately, so many do not appreciate these blessings and give themselves to passing joys. But real riches and blessings are found in the Son, as those who are with God understand. May they help us here below draw water from the fountain of life.

Soliloquy 14. Teresa exclaims whoever knows God loves God! But many do not want to know God. Those who look upon God in faith find God looks at them with love and draws them into communion. Those who turn away from God must face divine anger and judgment. Teresa remembers how she used to fear divine judgment and asks the Lord to preserve her in his love. Teresa prays that sinners may accept what the compassionate Lord and God offers to them. Why do so many people not understand what they are losing with their blindness.

Soliloquy 15. Teresa tells God how she finds this life so long as she waits for fuller union. Her longing is painful for she no longer finds happiness in anything in this world. She offers her intense longing to God, and accepts to live in this world as a sign of her desire to love God and do God's will in everything. The short time in this life seems so long but it is an opportunity to show God how deep is one's love.

Soliloquy 16. Teresa praises God's presence throughout the world and at times finds herself in painful longing to be with God. At times the vehemence of her love and the intensity of her painful longing produce wounds of love in the depths of her being. This separation has no human remedy, and only God whose absence causes this pain can heal it. This pain is so intense but also delightful, as every aspect of one's being unites in this experience of love.

Soliloquy 17. Teresa celebrates God's love for her—a love that loves her more than she can ever love herself. God knows her, understands her every need and desire, and does everything in and for her. All Teresa now desires is to do God's will, and she entrusts herself totally to God's designs for her. She longs to be with God and finds this short time on earth so long as she waits for it to end. God is blessed, our supreme Good, and offers intimacy to those who love what God loves and find joy in what brings God joy. Teresa longs to be a sharer in God's life and love. She places all her hope in God, longs to spend eternity in praise of God's mercies, and she wants to live and die in striving always for this life.

Comments on a few verses of the *Song of Songs*

In the middle ages and up to Teresa's time, the *Song of Songs* was the most commented book in the monasteries, and there were a series of commentaries from writers like William of St. Thierry, Bernard of Clairvaux, and others. Around the time of John of the Cross (1561), his teacher, Luis de León, prepared a new translation and wrote a commentary for his sister. In Teresa's time few men would have had the courage to write on this book given the opposition of the Spanish Inquisition, and even Luis of León was punished for his work. If men were reluctant, it was unthinkable that a woman would write on this book of Scripture, but Teresa chose to do so! Even so, her confessor at the time, Fr. Diego de Yanguas, ordered Teresa and her nuns to destroy all copies, not because he disagreed with the content, but precisely because he thought it was unsuitable for a woman to comment on this book. Fortunately, some copies were preserved.

Teresa's work is not a detailed commentary but a series of meditations on a few passages, and she even says that this is not an organized interpretation or commentary but the use of a few select passages as points of departure for some spiritual reflections. In fact, she uses just six short quotes which she may have heard in sermons or read in the little office of the Blessed Virgin—for she did not have access to the Bible in the vernacular. The earliest possible date for this work would be around 1566, since Teresa mentions two previous books which must have been the *Autobiography* (1656) and the *Way* (1566). The latest date would be around 1575 when Fr. Domingo Báñez approved the work. Some commentators speak of two drafts, one written around 1567 and the other around 1572-75.

Concerns about the appropriate use of the Song of Songs have been common throughout history, as one would expect, given the fact that this book of Scripture never mentions God once, does not deal with explicit religious issues, and is filled with erotic imagery. Many commentators chose to interpret it as an allegory or parable that dramatically describes God's love for humanity; the latter is the bride and the former the groom, while the "daughters of Jerusalem" become the world that looks on in awe at the relationship of love between God and humanity. Christians have also viewed the poem as describing the relationship between Christ and the Church, and in liturgy have suggested that the bride is Mary, either individually in her love for God's will or as a symbol of the Church in relation to Christ.

Chapter 1. Scripture as a source of inspiration and love.

Teresa recommends the reading of Scripture with awareness that it reveals mysteries of faith and we cannot understand everything fully. Biblical scholars must study the Scriptures and explain them to us. We should accept with simplicity the knowledge we gain but also be aware that at times God gives us deeper understanding without our efforts. The *Song of Songs* is particularly difficult to understand, and some people even avoid reading or listening to it. These false fears can block our access to the love of God and to how God blesses a person who loves—both revealed in these lines. These are great mysteries, spoken by the Holy Spirit, and they can enkindle love within us. Some people will never understand the mysteries contained in these verses, others are so enthralled by God's love they burst into praise when they hear them. Those who love can understand the love expressed in these lines and can appreciate the joys and delights that result from this love. We must never fail to do what we can for the love of God.

Teresa points out there is a lot she does not understand in the *Song of Songs*, but scholars, too, never exhaust its meaning. However, she finds consolation and a challenge to love in the lines and interprets the passages as best she can. She tells her readers they should do this with humility, fidelity to the Church, and check with learned people now and again. Teresa hopes her sharing with her readers will be helpful to them. The first words Teresa comments on are "Let him kiss me with the kiss of his mouth." She is frightened at the thought that a human being can say this to God, and concludes only a soul, mad with love, can say these words. A kiss is a sign of great friendship and peace, and the Lord has already shown us admirable signs of his love for us.

Chapter 2. False kinds of peace.

In the passage "Let him kiss me. . . " the bride is seeking peace, but there are all kinds of false experiences of peace. People who give themselves to evil living may think they live in peace, but they are simply not disturbed by evil around them and within them. Some people give in to small failures for so long they get accustomed to them and find a false peace. They become careless in little things, insensible to the growth of evil in their lives and in doing so find a false peace. Others may well be dedicated to prayer, but when they leave prayer they encounter all sorts of obstacles and disturbances, but seem to live calmly in an unreal peace in spite of their difficulties and do not seem to grieve over their faults. Habitual faults go ignored and they show no remorse—this false peace is dangerous.

Attachment to objects that this world values can lead to false peace. The possession of riches can also lead to false peace. Some have lots of money, enjoy it, and give to the poor, and they think all is well, and then they find a deceptive peace. This approach is not enough. The rich can become slaves to their wealth and forget they must give an account. Poverty is the Lord's gift and no account is needed for the gifts he makes to us. This can lead to true peace, while possessiveness and wealth lead to false peace. This world also values honors that can lead to false security and peace. Sometimes other people's praise of us can lead to harm if we are not careful. We must be watchful never to seek peace based on others' praise. This leads to a false sense of security and peace. If people praise us for virtue, we should humbly remember that virtue is God's gift. Teresa tells us to never trust others' praise, for it is not a source of peace. We must also remember that to seek peace in comforts is very dangerous. People who live very comfortably think they have peace, and they do not realize there is another world ahead of us. Their peace is deceptive. Sometimes people seek comfort under the excuse of sickness. Certainly discretion is important, but craving for comforts comes in many forms and it never brings peace.

True peace comes from friendship with the Lord. There are many levels of this friendship and sometimes ours is only shallow, and many of us could reach deeper levels of friendship. Let us develop big and courageous goals, for when we do the Lord will give us the grace for courageous deeds. We must persevere in these courageous thoughts and never slide back. This means self-control, making sure even small faults do not take root, and then we must pray that the Lord will help us develop real friendship, for without the Lord's help we can do very little.

There are many kinds of imperfect friendship with the Lord. First, God is so patient with us, compassionately waiting for our friendship to grow, but we are inconsistent and frequently fail in our response of friendship to the Lord. Second, some people build a strong friendship with the Lord based on never sinning seriously but they do not avoid lesser sins. In fact, they become careless, presuming on God's forgiveness. This kind of lukewarm friendship with the Lord is not enough. We must develop a pure conscience and pray for deeper friendship. Third, some are totally committed to the

Lord and seek never to offend him, but they allow themselves occasions that weaken their friendship. While their lives and prayer are good, they seek enjoyment and satisfaction in this world's pleasures, honor or respect, and even insisting on their own will. Anyone who wants to grow and live securely in peace must avoid this laxity. Fourth, Teresa mentions some who have given themselves to God, have avoided many forms of false peace and friendship, and even live in penance. However, they are attached to the honor or respect they think is their due and are always concerned about others' opinions of them. They seem to drag along behind them the cross of our Lord rather than loving it. Fifth, a final group of people is made up of those who avoid all the problems listed here but are not exercised in mortification and in denying their own wills. These faint-hearted people lack the courage, daring, and determination needed to receive the peace and friendship of the Lord.

Chapter 3. True peace is found in union with the Lord.

There comes a time when a dedicated person must endeavor to go beyond all the false forms of peace to seek union with the will of God—a union based on deeds with no self-interest. God has already shown us how much God loves us, and so we should no longer delay in our own total self-gift to God. After all, God shows us so many signs of love by the blessings he gives those who seek authentic peace and friendship. Moreover, there are signs of our commitment too. One sign is contempt for all worldly interests, another is never seeking one's own benefits, and another is rejoicing in the company of those who love God. At this point it is up to God to use us or not, in whatever ways God sees fit. Love and faith are now at work, and we will need to withstand all distractions of the intellect and all excuses for not progressing. But nothing is impossible to those who love. We need determination, strength, and humility so that we do not fall back into false forms of friendship. Some people will think our love is crazy, but in union with a so generous God we can achieve heroic deeds. We must pay no attention to fear, weakness, or discouragement, but remember God's overwhelming love and always seek true peace and friendship in union with God.

Chapter 4. The prayer of quiet and communion in friendship.

Commenting on the words of the *Song of Songs*, "Your breasts are better than wine. . .", Teresa speaks about how God communes with people in deep friendship and love. In a person's deepest center he or she experiences the nearness of God. In this prayer the faculties are under control, and so without distractions a person is in calm quiet, absorbed in the comfort the Lord gives. The Lord shows such a person how profoundly he loves him or her, insists that nothing separates the two, and shares special revelations. This experience leaves one with understanding, strength in virtue, and awareness of God's presence. One is absorbed in God, seems carried outside oneself, and yet understands something of what is happening. One feels suspended in the arms of the Lord and rejoices in the Lord's intimate communications. When this experience passes, one is left dazed, overwhelmed by the grandeurs of God, and endowed with unmerited delight. Teresa prays that others will gain a taste of the joys that come with this prayer of quiet and initial union, and also appreciate the suffering that comes with it. Union in love with the Lord is not reserved for the next life, but offered to us also in this present life. Teresa urges all to give themselves totally to God. God has loved us so much, gives us permission to love him in return and, in fact, he says he needs our love.

Chapter 5. The prayer of union and its blessings.

Teresa asks what shall be our response to these blessings of the Lord. We must stay close to the Lord and enjoy the nourishment and solace he gives us. After all, people who receive these special blessings have generally labored much in the Lord's service and striven to prepare themselves for his love; they are worn out with meditation and weary of the world and its values. Now, they just want to be with the Lord. In this prayer of quiet and union when the faculties are quiet and calm, they are engulfed in joy and blessings and feel protected by the Lord. No longer is there any need to work, as in meditation, for all that one does now is taste and enjoy the Lord in union. Everything now comes from God through the mediation of the Holy Spirit who enables a person to receive more, to grow more, and to focus all interests on God's love.

Chapter 6. The benefits of this loving union.

This prayer brings peace and satisfaction to the dedicated person. So much so that each one feels there is nothing more to seek or receive. But God still has so much more to give, beyond all our desires and expectations. God distributes further gifts with such overwhelming generosity people feel stunned at such intensity and liberality. These undeserved blessings, passively bestowed, when all senses and faculties are asleep, unite a person with God in love. When all the faculties have no interest except to be focused on the loving God, one becomes inebriated with love, and God receives this love and returns it, further enriched. The person feels beside himself or herself, suspended, and unaware of how this love works. However, one enjoys progress in prayer, virtues, faith, and contempt for the world's false values. We cannot explain these experiences rationally but appreciate them in awe, as we see the workings of God's love. God is happy when we reach this prayer of union and helps us to grow even more in love, bestowing unheard of blessings. At this point, a person does not know how nor understand what he or she loves, for God has accepted this love without the faculties' participation. God grants these favors sometimes after a short time and sometimes after a long time, as and when God designs. This union produces strong, boundless love for God and neighbor, along with transformation in life.

Chapter 7. Effects of this prayer of union.

Teresa describes the intense love experienced in this prayer, a love so strong a person wants to die to be with God in love. But in spite of this desire Teresa says a person in this stage desires to remain in this life in order to serve the Lord to whom he or she owes so much. In this prayer a person feels in suspension, unable to react, and feels death would be the best outcome, but also recognizes the Lord wants one to continue to live here in service to the Lord and to neighbors. Now the active and contemplative aspects of life go together. A person engages in the service of others without any self-interest, and is not limited by discretion and self-care, but does everything only for the love of God, and such service benefits many. Motivated by the intense love experienced in this prayer, one focuses on others' spiritual needs and does enormous good to others. Moreover, any suffering is willingly and lovingly accepted for it comes as a balance to prolonged suspension. So, the more one advances in this prayer, the more one pays attention to the needs of neighbors.

In this chapter we have read some of Teresa's works beyond the usual four major ones. The *Spiritual Testimonies*, *Soliloquies*, and *Comments on the Song of Songs* give us insights that contribute greatly to our appreciation of Teresa's spiritual life and find guidance for our own. There are other works, too, that fill us with appreciation for Teresa's many gifts. The *Constitutions* and directions "On Making the Visitation" show us Teresa's practicality and sense of balance as a Mother Foundress who can combine legislation, a healthy approach to austerity and the avoidance of extremes, and a constant dedication to seek the highest standards of spiritual life, both individual and communal. The two spiritual challenges give us a glimpse of Teresa's desire to involve others in a group response to spiritual questions, while also appreciating that this was often a form of enjoyable entertainment and recreation in monasteries of her time. Teresa's poetry is an extension of her spiritual life and also shows her joy in sharing special moments with her sisters, as well as using the poems for their spiritual formation. She must have written many more than we have. The ones we have deal with love, painful longings, contempt for worldly values, seeking God, surrender to God, joy in union with God, and gratitude for God's beauty, goodness, and blessings. Then there are some others on the Christmas season, the passion, feasts of saints, and celebrations of the religious ceremonies of her nuns. Finally, Teresa's large collection of letters, which is too extensive to deal with here, gives us insight into her overwhelming interest in others' needs, her extensive ministry activities, and some of the problems she had to deal with. Of course all these issues are punctuated with her spiritual values, interests, dedication, and love for the Lord.

A few final thoughts from Teresa

- Always be aware of the blessings God has given you and continues to give you. Let this awareness lead you to greater humility.
- Let the Lord and no one else teach you to pray, then you will make much progress in detachment and authentic freedom from anything that does not lead you to God.
- The Lord wants you to joyfully surrender yourself to him in peace and tranquility, in gratitude for the blessings you have received, and in awareness of God's love for you.
- God's love is permanent and unfailing, but often it takes years before you return this love. How can you recover this lost time?
- Accept with simplicity whatever the Lord gives you.
- Never seek peace except in the Lord. True peace will come to you when you seek only union with God's will, a union based on deeds with no self-interest.
- The more you advance in prayer the more you must pay attention to the needs of everyone around you.

Chapter Nine

Stages in the life of prayer

Teresa's life and teachings on prayer

We have seen that the stages of prayer proposed by St. Teresa come from her personal experiences and that they evolved over her life, giving rise to deeper insights as her own spiritual experience matured. The diagram below shows the stages in Teresa's own life and the appropriate mansion or stage in the spiritual life which she experienced at various periods in her life. I have also placed below the stages the major works of Teresa and the stages in prayer which they covered.

---------------Ascetical-------------- ----------------Mystical-----------------------

Childhood	Vocation .	Pre-mysti'l	Early union	Ecstasy	Total union	
1515	1531-32	1543-4	1554	1562	1572	1582
Mansions 1-3		Man 4	Man 5	Mansion 6	Mansion 7	

--WAY-------------------

           -------------LIFE--------------------

----------------------------------INTERIOR CASTLE-----------------------------

                --FOUND'NS---

In the *Autobiography*, Teresa presents prayer in four stages which she describes as four ways of bringing water to a garden.

1st water is meditative prayer

2nd water is the prayer of quiet

3rd water is the prayer of the sleep of the faculties

4th water is the prayer of union

In the *Interior Castle*, Teresa describes prayer in seven stages which she describes as deeper penetrations of the walls of a fortified city until one arrives at the very center, where his majesty the King dwells, or as seven sets of rooms within a wonderful mansion.

Mansion 1. Simple vocal prayer

Mansion 2. Occasional meditation

Mansion 3. Habitual meditation

Mansion 4. Prayer of quiet (reference to recollection, and allusion to sleep)

Mansion 5. Simple union

Mansion 6. Mystical engagement

Mansion 7. Mystical matrimony

In the *Way of Perfection*, Teresa does not give a series of stages but does refer to a simple method which she refers to as recollection or presence to the Lord in quiet and peace.

We should add to these stages Teresa's listing of degrees of prayer given in her 59th *Spiritual Testimony*, in which she gives some stages in prayer along with some experiences within the stages. In this testimony to her spiritual director, the Jesuit, Fr. Rodrigo Alvarez, Teresa lists the following:

Constant awareness of the presence of God

Interior recollection

Prayer of interior quiet and peace

The sleep of the faculties

The prayer of union

The prayer of ecstasy or suspension

Transport of the soul

Flight of the spirit

Impulse of love

Wounded with an arrow

Union with the Holy Trinity

Teresa's main descriptions are those in the *Autobiography* and *Interior Castle* and they show some clear relationships while keeping in account Teresa's own life development and especially her growing and maturing understanding of the development of prayer.

Waters	Life chps. 11-22	Interior Castle	Mansions
		Simple vocal prayer	1
I	Meditative prayer	Occasional meditation	2
		Habitual meditation	3
		Prayer of infused recollection	
II	Prayer of quiet	Prayer of quiet	4
III	Prayer of the sleep of the faculties	(Allusion to sleep)	
IV	Prayer of union	Simple union	5
		Mystical engagement	6
		Mystical matrimony	7

So, these stages relate to each other, as we see in the following diagram.

Relationship between the Four Waters of the *Life* (Life 11-22), the ascetical preparations in the *Way*, and the Seven Mansions of the *Interior Castle*:

Mansions	1.	2.	3.	4.	5.	6.	7.

Waters ("Life")		I		II&III	IV		

"Way"
Recollection,quiet,union

Active stages in the life of prayer

The point of departure for all spiritual growth is not us but God. We are not moving forward but being drawn forward. So, we are not moving from stage 1 to 2 to 3 and so on, struggling on our own until we reach stage 7. Rather, the point of departure is God who is the primary lover, totally interested in us moving to union in divine life and love. God is the point of departure and comes to our help, drawing us forward through stages 1, 2, and 3, blessing our contributions in the early stages of the spiritual life. This is what Teresa calls "my life." Then God takes over and grants the blessings of the later stages, drawing us to union; what Teresa calls "the life that God lived in me."

It has always been thought that there are two phases in spiritual life; an active phase and a passive phase. Both are God's blessings to us, but in the first phase our contributions and efforts are important even though our efforts primarily consist in getting out of God's way! We are learning how not be an obstacle to God's work within us. We begin our journey to God by learning three fundamental attitudes that must remain with us throughout our entire lives: love, detachment, and humility. Love is the defining characteristic of a Christian personality, and it can never be absent from anything we do. Detachment simply means we have no interest in anything except a God-directed life. However, every aspect of life must be a part of this, so every aspect of life needs to be integrated into our spiritual development. There is no such thing as religious and non-religious aspects of life; all must be part of our self-gift to God. Humility calls us to keep our feet on the ground ("humus" = earth), get to know ourselves well, be real in everything we do, and be true to ourselves. Religion and spiritual growth is the single best way to be human, to be who we are called to be. These are the three touchstones of spiritual authenticity—love, integration, and realism. Religious and mystical writers can, at times, let themselves be carried away with the language of love, can interpret detachment as self-rejecting approaches to life. These three qualities go together and are mutually sustaining and mutually corrective. Love must be integrative and real. Detachment must be loving and imply a real relationship with this world. Humility must be loving, even of oneself, and imply a real and authentic relationship with every aspect of life. Once these three foundational attitudes are a part of life, we can begin our journey to God, and as we do—with all our efforts—God transforms these efforts with charity, hope, and faith, so that we learn new ways of loving, possessing, and knowing.

Speaking of Teresa of Avila, one author comments, ". . . the more one reads her, the more keenly one feels that her mission in life was less to found Carmelite

convents than to help millions everywhere to live the
life of prayer."[12]

First stage of prayer—vocal prayer. (See
Autobiography, chps. 11, 12, 13; *Castle,* mansion 1)

We express our innermost being through our bodies
and our first form of prayerful expression is vocal prayer. This
can never be merely mechanical but must always be permeated
by thought, reflections, and as Teresa insists, always reflecting
on who is speaking to whom. This stage, along with the next
two, is part of the beginners' purification. We must purify our
negative energies, identify the obstacles we present, and
convince ourselves that we have to be different. It is a period
when we struggle to reject sin and a world of distractions to
pursue the life of grace. We need self-knowledge and humility,
and we must be content to be where we are and yet open to be
led. If we want this vocal prayer and reflection to be part of a
serious commitment to spiritual growth we will need a lot of
courage, even in this early stage. The problem is that any
interest in this world and its false values blocks our ability to
appreciate what lies ahead in the later stages, and we can easily
feel helpless and without ability to move ahead. Self-
understanding and humility are the dominant needs and
achievements of this first stage. Vocal prayer plus reflection is
an important first step in prayer. With this prayer we are
beginning to think about God and who God is for us; we are
reflecting on God's presence to us and our need to think about
a realm of life beyond this present one. When we immerse
ourselves in this prayer, we should choose a fixed time of
adequate length and subject matter that is inspiring.

Second stage of prayer—occasional meditation.
(See *Autobiography*, chps. 14, 15; *Castle*, mansion 2)

As we continue our vocal prayer with reflection, especially when our prayer forms include inspiring and challenging words and thoughts, it becomes natural enough that we think a little more, try to understand the words we are reciting, savor the sentiments, apply them to ourselves and to our world, and even make resolutions based on them. This step by step process of discursive thought and affective reaction is what we call meditation. At first it happens just now and again, as God uses our efforts to draw us forward. At this point we begin to focus more on truths we encounter in our reflective vocal prayer and especially to center our minds and hearts on the person of Jesus whom we find is accompanying us at every step. In this occasional meditation the Lord is encouraging us to understand spiritual truths and values, to learn more about ourselves and our faults and failings, and to enkindle our energy and affection for an increasingly present, loving God. Even in this early stage of prayer we find something is happening to our minds and our hearts. We also begin to appreciate that our faculties are focusing differently than previously.

Teresa comments on stage one—vocal prayer, using the allegory of a deaf-mute, and points out that we can neither hear the voice of God speaking to us nor can we speak to the Lord, for we are spiritually both deaf and dumb. In this second stage, Teresa suggests we are still dumb and unable to speak to the Lord, but we are no longer deaf, for we can hear the Lord's voice calling us. We understand and appreciate that the Lord is calling us, and this understanding encourages us to move on in our prayer. This makes the second stage more difficult than the first for we appreciate what we are missing. It is time to leave aside attachments to the false values of this world. We will face many temptations, and we need to be aware of the many dangers that beset us at this early stage. However, there will be failures, but we should not let them discourage us. As we deliberately meditate now and again, we find that we desire what the Lord wants for us, and this attitude is the basis for entrance into all the other mansions. We must maintain good desires and pray the Lord will endow us with perseverance.

Third stage of prayer—habitual meditation and acquired recollection. (See Autobiography, chps. 16, 17; *Castle*, mansion 3)

When we give ourselves to occasional meditation we more and more try to make a habit of it. Our small efforts and the attraction and blessings of God lead us to make regular meditation an important part of each day. We need to strengthen this commitment with good Christian living, avoidance of even venial sin, and a progressive effort to purify failings and re-educate our faculties and senses with self-sacrifice. A key characteristic of this stage is the practice of promptness in obedience to God's will as we begin to obey the demands of grace. Three developments happen to our meditation in stage three: 1. we increase our meditation until it becomes habitual, 2. we decrease the discursive and intellectual aspects of reflection and focus more on the affective dimensions of the concluding part of meditation, and 3. we simplify our meditation in active recollection. So, three components characterize stage three; habitual meditation, affective prayer, and the prayer of simplicity or active recollection.

As we give ourselves to habitual meditation, Teresa tells us that we should feel happy and free at this time, relax in recreation, and have confidence that we will grow. However, we should take care to use a knowledgeable spiritual director, to maintain humility without any pride or satisfaction in the growth of this stage, to emphasize our spirit of detachment, and to be aware of the importance of self-sacrifice and mortification. While endeavoring to make meditation habitual we must not prolong the discursive aspects but frequently stop in silence. It is also important that we choose good subjects for prayer, base our prayer solidly in Scripture, and avoid any and all foolish devotions. This third stage is one of special blessings for each of us, and we must take care that we do not expect others to be like us but always see the good in others.

Prayer is not what we are doing but what God is doing in us. We must become aware of our own potential in prayer. Our prayer must be able to overwhelm us with the happiness of faith and faith-filled love. Most of us live with only a shadow of what our prayer should be.

All meditation should end with acts of love of God— that is the reason for the discursive reflection, to stimulate the will to love. As we become more accustomed to the practice of meditation we decrease the preparatory reflective parts and increase the affective parts, so that the workings of the will take over from the discussions and reflections of the intellect. The more meditation develops, the more love takes over, and gradually we want to conform our will and our way of loving to Christ's.

As meditation becomes habitual and as affective prayer takes over, our meditation also becomes simpler, what Teresa refers to in the *Way of Perfection* (chp. 28) as acquired recollection. In this prayer we recollect our senses, look at the Lord and know he is present to us, and give him our simple, loving attention. Former reasoning and discursive prayer are transformed into a simple loving gaze on God. In this active recollection, which results from our own efforts, we gain a conscious realization of the presence of God. We should cultivate the habit of awareness of the presence of God and maintain companionship with God during the day. We do well to prepare our bodies in stillness, to quiet our minds in peace, to find a sacred space and sacred time, and to recollect, concentrate, and rest in the Lord. Then, we can attentively respond to the Lord, listening, sharing, and expressing our love. If our minds wander, we should try to re-collect ourselves and re-focus on being present to the Lord.

> "Our principal way of relating to God in prayer is to be open to receive. Our contribution amounts to removing obstacles of a false self, an inaccurate understanding of prayer, and a too-human perception of God. Our primary response is openness and receptivity, letting God transform us in every aspect of our being. The strategy of giving time to reflection and prayer is a decision for depth, enrichment, and transformation in our spiritual lives. Being constantly connected to God through prayer helps empty us of selfishness and brings us the power to be our true selves."[13]

Passive, mystical stages in God's gift of prayer

The second phase of prayer is the mystical or contemplative. This is a passive phase and these stages of prayer cannot be acquired. Rather they are completely gift from God. Mysticism refers to the hidden or inaccessible aspects of prayer that we can only encounter due to God's love and blessings. We do not earn contemplation, but God draws us to this new life if God so chooses and if we are prepared and made to have the capacity by God. In contemplation a person experiences that God is present to him or her. It is an immediate and direct contact with God even though it may not be felt or known. It can also be an experience that includes an intuition which is intense, profound, and very simple. In contemplation a person is moved passively by God. This is an experience which is not in words but in love, and so it is ineffable. It is an infusion of knowledge and love and is given in different ways and degrees to people who are particularly purified of self-centeredness, committed to love, and desire only to do the will of God. Contemplation has great sanctifying qualities. Contemplation leads to a renewal of life, to a wisdom in our knowledge of God, and to union with God in love. It is an enlightenment, an expansion of consciousness, and a great awakening. It produces forgetfulness of self, a desire to do God's will, and a commitment to the service of others. It brings a person inner peace, increased spiritual strength, and personal fulfillment. Contemplation is humanity's greatest opportunity to welcome God into life. This is the light that comes with darkness.

Clearly no one can earn the gift of contemplation, but we can prepare ourselves with the daily dedication to stillness of our bodies, to being open and attentive to the inspirations of the Holy Spirit, to lovingly concentrate on Christ, and to practice silence in God. We can do all this by fostering an awareness of the presence of God, a spirit of recollection, a sense of wonder, a healthy sense of aloneness, and the patience, and willingness to wait. All this takes place in the active phase of prayer, what we have seen in the first three stages. However, when all is said and done contemplation is a gift that purifies and transforms our ways of communicating with God, and prepares us for a loving union.

The fourth stage of prayer—the prayer of quiet (This prayer is preceded by the prayer of infused recollection and followed by the prayer of the sleep of the faculties). (See *Autobiography*, chps. 18, 19, 20, 21; *Castle*, mansion 4)

Teresa writes the *Interior Castle* about twelve years after the *Autobiography*, during which time her own spiritual experiences and her understanding of what was happening in prayer matured. Part of that maturing was to suggest that prior to the prayer of quiet there is another form of prayer (the first mystical stage she experienced) that almost always precedes the prayer of quiet, namely the prayer of recollection. She says that this part of the prayer of recollection is passive, gift, and cannot be acquired. This prayer of infused recollection leads into the prayer of quiet. So, with infused recollection or infused contemplation God's work within us intensifies. Our task at this time is not to be obstacles to God's grace. New knowledge, love, and inestimable blessings are re-collected by God in our deepest spirit. We do not know this wisdom, rather we experience it, as and when God chooses. God overwhelms us with divine presence and brings a new centering or interior re-collecting into the very depths of our spirits. A person feels he or she is losing hold on former reality. Even though faculties continue in their normal tasks, they are losing interest in all external things. In this early phase of the fourth mansion God is drawing us forward, awakening us to love, and inviting us to center all life on God alone. This prayer of infused recollection is the entrance into the prayer of quiet. We must not force this form of prayer but simply seek God and the divine will in everything. In this prayer we discover a new centering of our entire lives, and it prepares us for God's future gifts and transformation.

The prayer of quiet is God's work within us. It is a time when the major spiritual interventions of God begin, and a person gains a new experience and a new way of knowing God. On our part we need humility, charity, and continued care of the ascetical life. This is a prayer in which the will is passive but not the other faculties of intellect and memory, and it is important that we do not allow ourselves to be distracted by the faculties in such a way that they quench the spark of God's love and gifts. Teresa tells us not to think much at this time but to love much. This is a time when virtues grow and understanding deepens—signs of God's special blessings. A problem can arise because of these blessings, namely, many reach this stage, think it is the end, and few pass beyond it. This can also be a time of suffering, sometimes caused because we cannot understand what is happening to us. Teresa's advice is to remember that all the reason has to do is understand there is no reason! At this time, perhaps the one thing we can do is to make non-discursive acts of love and commitment.

In the prayer of quiet a person experiences extraordinary peace and pleasure in recognizing God's presence deep within one's inner spirit. It is as if one knows God is present, communicating knowledge and love. In fact, one feels captivated by God's personal presence, deep within one's spirit. At first, this experience may only last a few minutes, but it can also become frequent and eventually habitual. The will is passive, wanting nothing except to be in this loving and revealing presence. The intellect and memory are still active but more focused on the things of God. Teresa tells us that the prayer of quiet produces transforming effects in a person—he or she becomes different in spiritual life and commitment because of God's loving and revealing presence. Teresa gives the following effects of the prayer of quiet: liberty of spirit, desire never to offend God, profound confidence in God, dedication to suffering that comes from love, humility, a disdain for anything that does not lead to God, and a general growth in virtues. A person who is blessed with the prayer of quiet finds that nothing matters anymore, except to love in this intimate presence with God. This awareness permeates everything a person does.

Teresa also suggests in the *Autobiography* that the prayer of quiet with its passivity of the will can merge into a fuller experience of the passivity of all the faculties—what she calls the prayer of the sleep of the faculties. Previously, the faculties of intellect and memory might even distract a person in prayer, then they began to focus more on the things of God. Now at this time besides the will, the intellect too is passive while other faculties of memory and imagination retain the power to concentrate on God but can still distract the soul. This union of the entire person with God brings both pain and joy. It is a fuller union, but not total and the person retains awareness of being in this world.

This fourth stage in prayer begins with infused recollection which affects primarily our way of knowing God, moves to the prayer of quiet which affects principally the will, and concludes in the prayer of the sleep of the faculties in which all the faculties are at rest. The next step will be the prayer of union.

Fifth stage of prayer—prayer of simple union. (See *Castle*, mansion 5; *Spiritual Testimony* 25)

Teresa distinguishes three stages in the prayer of union, three progressive steps towards complete passivity of all faculties and union with God. They can be understood as three stages in spiritual marriage: courtship, engagement or betrothal, and marriage. The fifth stage in prayer, the prayer of simple union, is a progressive development from the increasing passivity of the faculties in the prayer of the sleep of the faculties when the main faculties of will and intellect are passive. Now, all the faculties are passive, totally centered on union with God—the will loves, the intellect is in awe at the love, and there is no memory at all, for all are in union with God. The soul has no further interest in the things of this world but abandons itself to God who takes possession of it. This experience of being totally captivated by the loving presence of God rarely lasts more than half an hour, but the person who experiences it can never doubt that it was an experience of union with God and moreover will never forget this experience for the rest of his or her life. As time passes the experience can prolong significantly. A particular difficulty experienced at this time is that since all the faculties are absorbed in the joy of the experience they cannot understand or communicate this experience. So, the joy is greater but less effectively expressed; it cannot be described, it must be experienced. The external senses are not totally captivated but seem at a loss to act in any determined way. So, in this prayer we no longer experience distractions, we become certain that this is an experience of God within us, and we find a new energy in pursuing the goal of union with God in love. Those who experience the prayer of union look at themselves and the world differently, sometimes like the silkworm, not fully understanding what has happened to them. Now life centers on fulfilling God's will in everything.

This stage of prayer leads to a transformation, but the person in this stage does not really understand what is happening; in fact, a person does not even recognize himself or herself. A person feels he or she is a different person, knowing he or she is now so united to God in love, in obedience to the divine will, and in complete service to others. Teresa suggests we think about a silkworm, born, crawling, eating, but that then weaves its own cocoon of death to former ways of living, and emerges as a butterfly. Teresa still considers that no matter how wonderful this prayer of union is, it is still just a courtship where two lovers are getting to know each other and trying to decide if they want to make this relationship permanent. This call to union is the fundamental purpose of life and each of us needs to reflect on our calling and ask for God's grace to be faithful.

As this prayer centers more and more on the celebration of God's transforming presence in the soul, it leads naturally enough to experiences that overwhelm the body and begin to produce signs of the body's disconnection to this world—this leads to experiences of suspension or ecstasy. These experiences that can begin in this stage are more evident in the next stage.

Sixth stage of prayer—ecstatic union. (*Castle,* mansion 6; *Spiritual Testimony 1, 2, 59*)

After the courtship of the prayer of simple union a person makes the final decision to be with his or her lover, pledging commitment and undertaking final preparations. Each wants the final transforming union of spiritual marriage to be as perfect as possible. One is naturally excited, beside himself or herself, and wanting to both enjoy the present peace and happiness in awareness of each other's love and commitment and also to prepare to be the best spouse possible. So, this is a period of intense enjoyment, some anxiety, and final preparations to become transformed and intimately united to each other. This sixth stage of prayer is a deepening of union of the entire person with God and an intense and painful purification in preparation for final union. The deepening union, sometimes called conforming union, is a development from stage five, in which not only the principal faculties but also even external senses are now passive to everything except God—one's entire being is now captivated by God. The key feature of this stage is absorption in God; all faculties and senses are now conformed to God. A person at this time is centered on God and has no interest in anything else, but will readily leave this intense union to go out in service to others when this is one's obligation and God's will. However, this can be painful when one's longing for God is so intense.

A consequence of this union of soul and body with God is the phenomenon of mystical ecstasy, or the state of suspension, when the person experiences himself or herself outside of the normal bodily reactions. Because of these experiences this sixth stage is called ecstatic union. Teresa speaks of ecstasy, including suspension, rapture, visions, and locutions—experiences of joy and divine revelation so intense that the body is carried out of itself. This can be followed by transport, which is beyond ecstasy and comes quickly and irresistibly and carries a person to a new level of being. Flight of the spirit is a profound communication of love, sometimes sudden and violent, in which a person escapes from his or her body and rises to God. An impulse of love refers to the experience of being filled with pain and longing for God. Furthermore, there is an experience of being wounded in one's heart with an arrow of love. All these experiences of deeper love sanctify and enrich the soul, revealing more about God in a short experience than in a lifetime of learning, but they also fill the soul with pain in feeling its unworthiness and longing. But God makes the soul personally feel the divine presence.

This experience of deeper union is accompanied by a deep and painful purification as a further preparation for final union. God achieves this transforming purification through contemplation. It is like the dark night in John of the Cross. Although the stages of the dark night are not as developed in Teresa's writings, she certainly had similar painful experiences of purification. The pain may come from others' misunderstanding and distrust, a feeling of loneliness, a fear of being abandoned by God or by friends, and a weariness from the intensity of the experience. Then, too, pain comes from unfulfilled longings for further union.

This sixth stage leaves a person overwhelmed by joy, peace, and contentment. It produces in the soul great detachment from all that is not God, creates within the soul a yearning for solitude, and encourages an intense desire to love and serve others in God's name. A soul willingly accepts the pain that comes with love. In this union of the entire soul with God the body shares in the delights of the soul. This is a special period of infused contemplation—a time of purification and growth in virtue and in love.

Seventh stage of prayer—transforming union. (*Castle*, mansion 7; *Spiritual Testimony* 13, 29, 31, 42, 46, 51, 53, 59)

Many writers, including Teresa, refer to this last stage as spiritual marriage because of their conviction that it is a permanent, indissoluble, state of love, and because the lover and God are made one in mutual surrender. This experience is also called transforming union because the lover is totally transformed in God. The ecstatic experiences are no longer present, trials may still occur, but above all this is a time of permanent peace, a time to experience the full power of God's love, and a time of total immersion and experience of the life and indwelling of the Trinity. Theologians consider that this is a time of confirmation in grace, which does not exclude smaller failings and sins which are part of a just person's daily life. This experience of transforming union in spiritual marriage leads to complete self-forgetfulness for the lover, a readiness to suffer the pains of love, peace in persecution and trials, a great desire to serve others, and a total integration of everything one does in loving gift to God.

For Teresa this final stage in prayer is particularly focused on a vision of the Holy Trinity and their indwelling in her soul. She lives in the presence and company of the Trinity and enjoys their nearness and intimacy. This experience of union is now permanent.

Contemporary challenges of Teresa of Avila

1. Teresa tells her readers that from the early stages in the spiritual life it is important always to desire what the Lord wants of you; this is fundamental for entrance into all stages in prayer. Teresa insists that the greatest block to growth in prayer is the lack of humility.

2. Prayer is not a movement from one stage to another, but the integrated development of vocal, meditative, and contemplative prayer. Be content where you are in the spiritual life, and yet be open to be led. However, in all your efforts you must never be discouraged.

3. Mary Magdalen and the Samaritan woman are models of prayer for Teresa; they spend time with the Lord, but in both cases their response to him leads to action.

Conclusion

The contemporary challenge of Teresa of Avila

1. Our times need visionaries who can help us reinvent our spiritual vision and dedication. Teresa is *a visionary saint* who has personally succeeded in spiritual life and can also teach us. Moreover, she has a very common sense approach to prayer that is appealing to ordinary people, seeking spiritual growth.

2. Teresa was over forty before she made a resolute commitment to respond to God's call within her. In her experience of discovery of God's call and her slow and at times reluctant giving of herself to God, we find *someone with whom we can identify*.

3. Fortunately for us Teresa shares with honesty and simplicity the ups and downs of her life and the gradual process of growth in her dedication to God. *She is so real to us in her struggles*; Teresa like us struggled for years in her

spiritual growth, at times half-hearted, lukewarm, and reluctant. She struggled so much, but eventually she gained the goals she sought. In doing so she becomes a model for us in our spiritual journey.

4. Teresa was a very busy woman, immersed in business transactions, national travel, complicated and tension-filled interactions. Yet she was *able to maintain spiritual dedication amidst the challenges of a very busy life.*

5. In spite of her slow start and years of set-backs, Teresa becomes a spiritual guide for us all, *a renowned teacher of prayer,* and a doctor of the universal Church. She teaches prayer step by step, showing us what we can do and how we can open our hearts to receive the graces of the Lord and to let the Lord draw us to himself. Because of her experiences she has become a great teacher of prayer for us all.

6. While focused on the goal of union with God in love, Teresa is also *concerned with teaching preparations for prayer* that each of us can undertake. She gives three qualities that are foundational for anyone who wishes to follow the way of prayer, qualities that are basic to all human, Christian development. They are first, love for one another; two, detachment from all created things as ends in themselves; and three, true humility, which is the main quality and must permeate the other two.

7. Teresa is truly an exceptional person who *fills us with enthusiasm for the spiritual journey.* She was a real person, filled with excitement in her commitment to God, and she became a marvelous instrument in God's hands.

8. Teresa was a very active person, in many ways in control of the practicalities of daily life. However, once *Teresa learned to let go and to surrender,* she became more alive than ever. When she changed the focus of her life from herself to God

great things happened to her and to her service and love of the Lord and of others.

9. *St. Teresa is a gift of God to the Church*; a saint who knows how to respond in times of post-conciliar renewal. Her spiritual life parallels the reforms of the Council of Trent. When Martin Luther doubted the inner transformation in grace, Teresa showed us what inner transformation looks like. When we are often surrounded by so much doubt, Teresa tells us simply and clearly that she has seen God, that she has experienced God's transforming action in her life.

10. Throughout the important periods of spiritual growth, Teresa was surrounded by a small group of confessors and guides who become disciples in pursuit of the mystical life of prayer. They form a community, a little Church, and they enable Teresa's writings, protect them for the larger Church, and so *Teresa's writings become a gift* of their Church to ours.

11. Teresa gives us *a spirituality that is amazingly modern*; it is filled with strength and determination, common sense, unflinching realism, and a keen sense of devotion. Teresa is a woman with a balanced personality that attracts the modern person in search of God.[14]

12. Teresa *teaches us to live in a real Church* with its strengths and weaknesses, benefiting from its gifts and struggling with its problems, pursuing its grace-filled life and burdened by its power struggles.

13. Called to mystical life and to profound union with God, Teresa insists on two components of one's spiritual life that are more important than all others—*commitment to the will of God at all times and to the love and service of others.*

Endnotes

1. See the diagram of the stages in Teresa's life and prayer in chapter nine.

2. Karl Rahner, *The Practice of Faith*, edited by Karl Lehmann and Albert Raffelt (New York: Crossroad, 1984), p. 22.

3. Herricks, quoted by Allison Peers, *Complete Works of St. Teresa of Avila*, Vol. 1. Introduction, p. xxxviii.

4. Louis de León, quoted in Elias Rivers, "The Vernacular Mind of St. Teresa," *Carmelite Studies*, 1984: 127.

5. E. Allison Peers, *Mother of Carmel*, New York: Morehouse-Gorham Co., 1946. p. 47.

6. Elizabeth Hamilton, *The Life of St. Teresa of Avila* (New York: Charles Scribner's Sons, 1959), p. 65.

7. Susan Muto, "St. Teresa of Avila: A Directress of Formation for All Times," *Carmelite Studies*, 1984: 5.

8. Kieran Kavanaugh, OCD. *The Way of Perfection*, Study Edition (Washington, DC: ICS Publications, 2000), pp. 23-24.

9. Steven Payne, "The Tradition of Prayer in Teresa and John of the Cross," in *Spiritual Traditions for the Contemporary Church*, Robin Maas and Gabriel O'Donnell, eds. (Nashville: Abingdon Press, 1990), p. 242.

10. Eamon R. Carroll, "The Saving Role of the Human Christ for St. Teresa," *Carmelite Studies*, 1984, p. 135

11. Carole Slade, *St. Teresa of Avila: Author of a Heroic Life* (Berkley, CA: Univ. of California Press, 1995), pp. 1-2.

12. Allison Peers, *Mother of Carmel*, p. 82.

13. Leonard Doohan, *Ten Strategies to Nurture Our Spiritual Lives*, 2015, p. 29.

14. Allison Peers, *Mother of Carmel*, p. 53.

Bibliography

Allison Peers, E. *Complete Works of St. Teresa of Avila*, Vol. 1. London: Sheed and Ward, 1946.

Allison Peers, E. *Mother of Carmel*, New York: Morehouse-Gorham Co., 1946.

Carroll, Eamon. "The Saving Role of the Human Christ for St. Teresa," *Carmelite Studies*, 1984: 133-151.

Doohan, Leonard. *Ten Strategies to Nurture Our Spiritual Lives*, 2015.

Hamilton, Elizabeth. *The Life of St.Teresa of Avila.* New York: Charles Scribner's Sons, 1959.

Kavanaugh, Kieran, OCD. *The Way of Perfection* (Study Edition). Washington, DC: ICS Publications, 2000.

Muto, Susan. "St. Teresa of Avila: A Directress of Formation for All Times." *Carmelite Studies*, 1984: 3-18.

Payne, Steven. "The Tradition of Prayer in Teresa and John of the Cross," in *Spiritual Traditions for the Contemporary Church*, Robin Maas and Gabriel O'Donnell, eds. Nashville: Abingdon Press, 1990, pp. 235-258.

Rahner, Karl. *The Practice of Faith.* Edited by Karl Lehmann and Albert Raffelt. New York: Crossroad, 1984.

Rivers, Elias. "The Vernacular Mind of St. Teresa," *Carmelite Studies*, 1984: 113-129.

Slade, Carole. *St. Teresa of Avila: Author of a Heroic Life.* Berkley, CA: Univ. of California Press, 1995.

OTHER BOOKS BY LEONARD DOOHAN

STUDIES OF THE MAJOR WORKS OF JOHN OF THE CROSS

This series presents introductions to each of the great works of John of the Cross. Each volume is a study guide to one of John's major works and gives all the necessary background for anyone who wishes to approach this great spiritual writer with appropriate preparation in order to reap the benefits of one of the most challenging figures in the history of spirituality. Each book is a complete introduction offering background, history, knowledge, insight, and theological and spiritual analysis for anyone who wishes to immerse himself or herself into the spiritual vision of John of the Cross.

While targeted to the general reader these volumes would be helpful to anyone who is interested in the spiritual guidance of this saint. These books give insight into the critical components of spiritual life and can be helpful for anyone interested in his or her own spiritual journey. They could be helpful for the many people involved in the spiritual guidance of others, whether in spiritual direction, retreat work, chaplaincy, and other such ministries. Throughout these books the reader is encouraged to develop the necessary attitudes, enthusiasm, spiritual sensitivity, and contemplative spirit needed to benefit from these spiritual masterpieces of John of the Cross. Attentive reflection on these studies will encourage readers to have a genuine love for John of the Cross and his approach to the spiritual journey.

These books give historical, regional, and religious background rarely found in other introductory books on John of the Cross. They each present an abbreviated and accessible form of John's great works. Later chapters in each book give John's theological and spiritual insights that could be used for personal reflection and group discussion. Sections abound in quotes and references from John's books and each sub-section can be used as the basis for daily meditation. The volumes complement each other, and together give the reader excellent foundation for reading the works of this great spiritual leader and saint.

Volume 1. John of the Cross: Your Spiritual Guide

This unique book is written as if John of the Cross is speaking directly to the reader. It is a presentation by John of the Cross of seven sessions to a reader who has expressed interest in John's life and teachings. This book introduces the great mystic and his teachings to his reader and to all individuals who yearn for a deeper commitment in their spiritual lives and consider that John could be the person who can guide them.

Table of contents

6. Necessary attitudes during the spiritual journey
7. Celebrating the goal of the spiritual journey

Volume 2. The Dark Night is Our Only Light: A Study of the Book of the *Dark Night* by John of the Cross

This introduction to the *Dark Night of the Soul* by John of the Cross gives all the necessary background for anyone who wishes to approach this great spiritual work with appropriate preparation in order to reap the benefits of one of the most challenging works in the history of spirituality. The book starts with the life of John of the Cross, identifying the dark nights of his own life. It provides the needed historical, religious, and personal background to appreciate and locate its content. It then presents readers with aids they can use to understand the work. With these preparations in mind the book moves on to present the stages of the spiritual life and the importance of the nights. A summary of John's own work brings readers in direct contact with the challenges of the message and its application today. The book ends with 20 key questions that often arise when someone reads this book.

Table of contents

Volume 3. The Spiritual Canticle: The Encounter of Two Lovers. An Introduction to the Book of the *Spiritual Canticle* by John of the Cross

The book starts with the life of John of the Cross, showing how he was always a model of love in his own life, and how, guided by his own experience he became a teacher and later a poet of human and divine love. The book provides the needed historical, religious, and personal background to appreciate and locate its content. The book then presents the links between John's *Spiritual Canticle* and Scripture's love poem, the *Song of Songs*. A summary of John's own work brings readers in direct contact with the challenges of the message and its application today. With these preparations in mind the book moves on to present the stages of the spiritual life and the importance of the journey of love. The book then focuses on key concepts in the *Spiritual Canticle*, applying each of them to contemporary situations. Finally it considers the images of God presented in the book and how they relate to the spiritual journey.

Table of contents

Volume 4. John of the Cross: The Living Flame of Love

The *Living Flame of Love* is the final chapter in John's vision of love. It describes the end of a journey that began in longings of love that became an experience of purification for the person seeking union. *The Living Flame of Love* picks up from the final stage of union in the love of spiritual marriage and describes, in great beauty, several aspects of this final stage in the union of love. All these ideas are part of John's wonderful vision of love. Many writers have emphasized the spiritual value of a life of love, but John's vision is more expansive and integrated than approaches presented by anyone else.

Table of contents

LEONARD DOOHAN

A Year with St. John of the Cross

365 Daily Readings
and Reflections

A Year with St. John of the Cross: 365 Daily Readings and Reflections

This book, *A Year with St. John of the Cross*, offers 365 daily readings and reflections. In this year with St. John of the Cross we will read and reflect on his life, ministry, spiritual direction, spirituality, as well as selections from all his works, short and long. The readings and reflections in this book will introduce readers to all these, as well as comments from many leading writers and commentators on John. This year will be an opportunity for readers to immerse themselves in the spirituality of John of the Cross. Each day offers a focused reading, four key reflections, and three specific challenges for the day.

For those who are enthusiastic supporters of St. John of the Cross, and for others who wish to discover new and substantial paths in their spiritual journey, this book is a one-of-a-kind opportunity to encounter John and his challenges like never before. Let your reading of this new book be your personal journey with John of the Cross, to a deeper union with God. One of the main uses of the book is to help readers who do not have ready access to a spiritual director. Maybe these readings and reflections will help. I hope you will find this special book helpful in your spiritual journey.

The One Thing Necessary: The Transforming Power of Christian Love.

This radical new interpretation of love as the touchstone of the Christian message, explores the human longing for meaning; the Scriptures; the relational model of the Trinity: the ideas of human vocation, destiny and community; the mystical spiritual traditions; and his own experiences to explain what love is, how we find it, and how it can change the world. Each of the seven chapters contains several quotes and focus points at the beginning and provocative questions at the end for reflection or discussion by adult religious education and bible study groups.

"This book is all about love—and love as the one thing necessary. It is most certainly not about easy love or cheap grace. It is about the transforming power of Christian love. It is not only challenging but disturbing, a book written with conviction and passion."

Fr. Wilfrid Harrington, OP., Biblical scholar.

"[Doohan's] artful gathering and arranging of ideas reminds one of the impact of a gigantic bouquet of mixed flowers chosen individually and with great care." **Carol Blank**, Top 1000 reviewers, USA.

"Would that we heard more about this in our churches and religious discussions because, "this transforming power of Christian love will save the world" (p. 93). **Mary S. Sheridan**, "Spirit and Life."

THREE BOOKS ON SPIRITUAL LEADERSHIP

How to Become a Great Spiritual Leader: Ten Steps and a Hundred Suggestions

This is a book for daily meditation. It has a single focus—how to become a great spiritual leader. It is a book on the spirituality of a leader's personal life. It presumes that leadership is a vocation, and that it results from an inner transformation. The book proposes ten steps that individuals can take to enable this process of transformation, and a hundred suggestions to make this transformation real and lasting. It is a unique book in the literature on leadership.

This book is the third in a series on leadership. The first, *Spiritual Leadership: The Quest for Integrity* gave the foundations of leadership today. The second, *Courageous Hope: The Call of Leadership*, gave the contemporary characteristics and qualities of leadership. This third book focuses on the spirituality of the leader.

Courageous Hope: The Call of Leadership

This book's focus on leadership and hope is very appropriate given today's climate of distrust that many find results in a sense of hopelessness in their current leaders. Individuals and organizations are desperate for leaders of hope. Many books on leadership point to the need for inner motivation, but that inner motivation must be hope in new possibilities for a changed future. It is hope that gives a meaningful expression to leadership and enables the leader to be creative in dealing with the present. More than anything else it is a vision of hope that can excite and empower leaders to inspire others to strive for a common vision.

"Doohan strengthens our resolve. He restores our hope. And in an echo of Robert Frost, he is not only a teacher, but an awakener. May this book find you in a place where your will to grow is matched by an inner radiance to serve and help heal those around you... the reading will meet you there and the end result will be a gift to the world." **Shann Ray Ferch, PhD., MFA** Professor and Chair, Doctoral Program in Leadership Studies, Gonzaga University. Editor, International Journal of Servant Leadership.

"Read every word of this book. Leaders stuck in the past, afraid to face the future, afraid to take a risk because they might be wrong need an infusion of *Courageous Hope*. People are not looking for a simple, blind-faith hope. They are looking for leaders with a deeper understanding of hope as described in this book." **Mary McFarland, PhD.,** Professor, and Former Dean of undergraduate through doctoral programs in Leadership. International consultant in leadership and education.

"Ask people who were alive during the Great Depression what a huge difference Franklin Roosevelt made in their lives by giving them reasons to be hopeful. Ask people who were alive during the papacy of John XXIII what they loved most about him, and chances are they'll say that "good Pope John" gave them hope for the future. Read Courageous Hope and learn how to be that kind of leader yourself." **Mitch Finley,** Author of over 30 award winning books.

Spiritual Leadership: The Quest for Integrity

In eight clear and challenging chapters, the reader is invited to partake of a rich menu of reflections on the meaning of spiritual leadership and how it can transform one's role in the workplace, ensuring a collaborative environment of trust and confidence that energizes not only the culture of an organization, but also the effective accomplishment of its mission.

Leonard Doohan's highly readable book presents leadership as a call motivated by faith and love that results in a change of life, a conversion, and a breakthrough to a new vision of one's role in the world.

"Leonard Doohan's *Spiritual Leadership* is a profound and caring work . . . I highly recommend it to anyone interested in the spiritual meaning of servant leadership." **Larry C. Spears.**

"'The leader within,' . . . is well served by Leonard Doohan's book, *Spiritual Leadership*. It is a profound guidebook for leaders of the future, who live their values, who keep the faith." **Frances Hesselbein.** Chairman, Leader to Leader Institute

"Dr. Leonard Doohan's new volume on Spiritual Leadership reaches beyond, or perhaps better, beneath the many current volumes on leadership which emphasize skill sets, techniques, and learned habits." **Robert J. Spitzer, SJ, PhD.** President and CEO, Magis Institute

TWO BOOKS ON CONTEMPORARY SPIRITUALITY FOR CHRISTIAN ADULTS

Embrace the new enthusiasm in the Church and nurture your Christian commitment with weekly reflection.

A new spirit is stirring in the Church. We must overcome the failures of the past and prepare ourselves for a future of growth and responsibility. Let us rekindle spiritual insight, accept our spiritual destiny, and refocus on the essential teaching of salvation. While many have left the institutional churches, and sadly may never return, perhaps the challenge to renewal of Pope Francis may re-attract them to the essentials of Christian commitment. The Church will grow and benefit from an informed laity who deepens knowledge of the essential teachings of faith. I created a book with short sections, targeting areas of personal reflection valuable for individuals and discussion groups for this purpose. Read a section each week and gain a new strategy for nurturing your spiritual life.

Rediscovering Jesus' Priorities.

This book urges readers to look again at Jesus' teachings and identify the major priorities. It is a call to rethink the essential components of a living and vital Christianity and a challenge to rediscover the basic values Jesus proclaimed. Use the book for a short meditation and personal examination, as a self-guided retreat to call yourself to renewed dedication to Jesus' call, or for group discussion and renewed application of Jesus' teachings.

Ten Strategies to Nurture Our Spiritual Lives: Don't Stand Still—Nurture the Life Within You.

This book presents ten key steps or strategies to support and express the faith of those individuals who seek to deepen their spirituality through personal commitment and group growth. These ten key components of spirituality enable dedicated adults to bring out the meaning of their faith and to facilitate their spiritual growth. It offers a program of reflection, discussion, planning, journaling, strategizing, and sharing.

All books are available from amazon.com

Comment on the author's blog at
johnofthecrosstoday.wordpress.com

Visit the author's webpage at
leonarddoohan.com

www.ingramcontent.com/pod-product-compliance
Lightning Source LLC
LaVergne TN
LVHW051510080426
835509LV00017B/2006